WITHDRAWAL

WITHDRAWAL

Rethinking Children and Research

Companion Website available

The Companion Website relating to this book is available online at:
http://education.kellett.continuumbooks.com

Please visit the link and register with us to receive your password and
access to the Companion Website.

If you experience any problems accessing the Companion Website,
please contact Continuum at info@continuumbooks.com.

Also available from Continuum

Respecting Childhood, Tim Loreman

Whose Childhood Is It?, Richard Eke, Helen Butcher and Mandy Lee

Education and Construction of Childhood, David Blundell

Other books in the *New Childhoods* series

Rethinking Childhood, Phil Jones

Rethinking Children and Families, Nick Frost

Rethinking Children's Rights, Phil Jones and Sue Welch

Rethinking Children, Violence and Safeguarding, Lorraine Radford

Rethinking Children's Play, Fraser Brown and Michael Patte

Rethinking Children and Research

Attitudes in Contemporary Society

Mary Kellett

New Childhoods Series

continuum

Continuum International Publishing Group
The Tower Building   80 Maiden Lane
11 York Road   Suite 704, New York
London SE1 7NX   NY 10038

www.continuumbooks.com

British Library Cataloguing-in-Publication Data
A catalogue record for this book is available from the British Library.

ISBN: 9781847063236 (paperback)
       9781441129130 (hardcover)

Library of Congress Cataloging-in-Publication Data
Kellett, Mary, 1955-
Rethinking children and research / Mary Kellett.
   p. cm.
ISBN 978-1-84706-323-6 – ISBN 978-1-4411-2913-0
1. Children–Research. 2. Child development–Research. I. Title.

HQ767.85.K45 2009
305.231072–dc22   2009034868

Typeset by Newgen Imaging Systems Pvt. Ltd, Chennai, India
Printed and bound in Great Britain by the MPG Books Group

This book is dedicated to Yvonne Perret
for her inspiring support of so many children

With thanks to Phil Jones for his critical reading of draft work

Contents

Introduction to New Childhoods Series

The amount of current attention given to children and to childhood is unprecedented. Recent years have seen the agreement of new international conventions, national bodies established, and waves of regional and local initiatives all concerning children.

This rapid pace has been set by many things: from children themselves, from adults working with children, from governments and global bodies. Injustice, dissatisfaction, new ideas and raw needs are fuelling change. Within and, often, leading the movement is research. From the work of multinational corporations designed to reach into the minds of children and the pockets of parents, through to charity-driven initiatives aiming to challenge the forces that situate children in extreme poverty, a massive amount of energy is expended in research relating to children and their lives. This attention is not all benign. Research can be seen as original investigation undertaken in order to gain knowledge and understanding through a systematic and rigorous process of critical enquiry examining 'even the most commonplace assumption' (Kellett, 2005, 9). However, as Kellett has pointed out, the findings can be used by the media to saturate and accost, rather than support, under-12s who are obese, for example, or to stigmatize young people by the use of statistics. However, research can also play a role in investigating, enquiring, communicating and understanding. Recent years have seen innovations in the focus of research, as political moves that challenge the ways in which children have been silenced and excluded result in previously unseen pictures of children's experiences of poverty, family life and community. The attitudes, opinions and lived experiences of children are being given air, and one of the themes within this book concerns the opportunities and challenges this is creating. As this book will reveal, research is being used to set new agendas, to challenge ways of living and working that oppress, harm or limit children. It is also being used to test preconceptions and long-held beliefs about children's lived experiences, the actual *effects* rather than the adult's *opinions* of the way parents see and relate to their children, or the actual impact of services and their ways of working with children.

In addition to the *focus* of research, innovations are being made in the *way* research is conceived and carried out. Its role in children's lives is changing. In the past much research treated children as objects: research was done on them, with the agenda and framework set purely by adults. New work is emerging where children create the way research is conceived and carried out. Children act as researchers, researchers work with questions formulated by children or work with children by a rights perspective.

This series aims to offer access to some of the challenges, discoveries and work-in-progress of contemporary research. The terms 'child' and 'childhood' are used within the series in line with Article 1 of the United Nations Convention on the Rights of the Child which defines 'children' as persons up to the age of eighteen. The books offer opportunities to engage with emerging ideas, questions and practices. They will help those studying childhood, or living and working with children to become familiar with challenging work, to engage with findings and to reflect on their own ideas, experiences and ways of working.

Phil Jones
Leeds Metropolitan University
completed Makweti, South Africa
November 2008

Author note: In this book the term 'children' is used to denote legal minors aged 0–18. The terms 'young people' and 'children and young people' are also used at various times where a social construction terminology is felt to be more appropriate.

Part 1
Issues, Debates and Challenges

Introduction

What does it mean to be a child in the twenty-first century?

We have all been children once but this does not mean we understand what it is to be a child in the first decade of the twenty-first century. The mechanics of growing up, of negotiating rites of passage may bear some similarities but the contexts are entirely different. A driver of a Morris minor in the 1950s could not immediately jump into a Toyota yaris in 2009 and manoeuvre his or her way around the M25 – there might be two cars involved but the road conditions are entirely different. Perhaps the first thing we have to do, therefore, when rethinking what it means to be a child in the twenty-first century is to acknowledge that we have much to learn. McDonald (2007) observed that policy making and children's views are often mismatched because they rely on constructions of childhood that do not accurately represent what a child is.

The politics of change and uncertainty give rise to contemporary childhoods which are shorter and more transient than ever. Residential mobility, neighbourhood disintegration and gentrification fuel transience (Hartas, 2008) which has a significant impact on the nature of contemporary childhoods.

Large, out of town retail parks are replacing local shops, distant theme parks are replacing community leisure spaces and parents' places of work are moving further from their homes. This has resulted in children's environments being located less and less in the physical context of a neighbourhood which in turn limits aspects of social cohesion. Risk-averse societies are restricting children's spaces and movement, the home and car absorbing most of this, leaving little opportunity for children to engage in adult-free recreation. Children are creating new worlds in cyberspace where they can escape into virtual zones that have less adult regulation and interference. Cyberspace is radically changing the nature of children's social interaction and friendships. In the UK, the private nature of family life is giving way to an ever more public regime of scrutiny and regulation.

Twenty-first century children are growing up in an era of radical doubt where the certainties of tradition are rejected and knowledge is contested (Parker, 1997). In our postmodern era, the expression of uncertainty is more challenging than accepting objective truths based on universal laws. This is because acceptance of objective truth removes all trace of personal responsibility. In expressing uncertainty we demonstrate a willingness to grapple with different perspectives and discourses – and take responsibility for them. Childhoods are changing, what it is to be a child is changing and now is a good time to rethink how we are responding.

Why do we need to rethink children and research?

A crucial source of knowledge and understanding about childhoods and children's lives comes from research. As the nature of childhoods evolves so the way we undertake research about children must evolve too. Early ethnographic studies taught us much about different childhoods and transitions to adulthood. Developmental psychology instructed us about cognitive processes and conditioned behaviour. Sociological studies encouraged a shift towards a perspective that childhoods are socially constructed. But not all research involving children has been good and, at times, significant harm has been perpetrated against children in the name of research. The rise of ethics as a driving force in research has begun to safeguard children from injurious practice. Recent years have witnessed a radical re-positioning of research involving children. James et al. (1998) steered our thinking away from children as objects of research to participating subjects who are social actors in their own right. The focus shifted from research 'on' children to research 'with' children and ultimately widening this focus to include research 'by' children (Kellett, 2005a). Such a re-positioning affects *all research* involving children. This book explores how different models of research have engaged with these paradigm shifts and the beneficial effects this is having on children's lives and on our understanding of childhood. Indeed on the nature and role of research itself.

A new wave of children's rights activity also shifted the topical foci of research away from cognition and behaviour towards concerns about children's wellbeing and lived experiences. The social inclusion movement extended this thinking to *all* children and challenged the notion of childhood as a homogenous entity. Children's right to be involved in decisions affecting their lives was established as a fundamental human right in the articles of the United Nations Conference on the Rights of the Child (1989). This energized a surge of participatory and voice initiatives that propelled children into the research arena with a new agency. The incidence of children as participant and co-researchers has grown and ethical considerations, particularly consent issues, have had to be re-worked to accommodate the changes. In due course children themselves were empowered to decide research agendas and lead their own investigations. The rapidity with which these changes have taken place suggests it is a good time to take stock and rethink children and research.

The aim of this book is to re-examine some of the research involving children from a historical perspective, use the lessons we can learn from such a scrutiny to project forwards and rethink how research can best serve present and future generations of children. There could not be a more pressing time to do this. Some are arguing that childhood is in crisis and heading for toxicity (a reference to how the modern world is damaging childhoods) and although not all would agree with this, most would acknowledge that children growing up in the twenty-first century face many new and complex challenges. By 2020 childhood depression is predicted to be the second highest cause of disability (World Health Organisation, 2001). According to a report by the Information Centre for Health and Social Care (2007) more than 4,000 children under 14 in the UK attempted to take their own life in a single year. Happiness, which is fundamental to children's wellbeing, is more and more seen through a lens of consumerism. Success is measured by narrow normative testing which leaves little room for the celebration of achievement.

An emphasis on the importance of children as 'beings' not 'becomings' and their entitlement to childhood as a human right has given a new prominence to children's citizenship. Children are citizens from the day they are born and practices have to adapt to nurture the citizenship skills they need. If children are to influence decision-making they need to develop capacity for judgement, for communicating their views and agency for action. These skills are not sufficiently reflected in current education systems.

> An ethical praxis framework is likely to support children to challenge inequality, participate in decision-making, exercise responsibility and respect and develop citizenship. Feelings, views, laws, social and cultural norms and notions of equality may deviate from interpretations of ethics. Thus, it is important for children to develop capacities to re-examine the standards of equality, care, justice, respect and citizenship to ensure that they are reasonable, based on local knowledge which takes into account the culture and the social-political reality of their life. (Hartas, 2008, 125)

Throughout this book the pivotal position of research *by* children is stressed. Accepting children as researchers in their own right promotes their democratic involvement in all phases of decision-making. Children obtaining knowledge about childhood situations from their insider perspective has the potential for change and transformation. By leading their own research and actively interrogating their own evidence they are able to offer informed views about social practices affecting their lives. Perhaps one of the most important axles driving this rethinking of children and research is the importance of researching difference. Researching difference challenges assumptions that underpin human variation and must necessarily challenge theoretical and methodological assumptions that underpin constructions of childhood. Children and young people researching difference offers another dimension to childhood research that empowers and emancipates marginalized groups, richly enhancing our knowledge and understanding.

How is this book organized?

This book is part of a series entitled New Childhoods edited by Phil Jones. Each volume takes an aspect of children's lives and rethinks what this means in contemporary society. This book focuses on a reappraisal of children and research. Research, in this context, is any kind of research whether it is on, with or by children.

The book is organized into three parts. Part 1 defines the issues and debates about child research and includes a historical overview charting the main changes and paradigm shifts of recent decades. It also looks at some of the critical issues of research involving children, particularly ethics. Part 2 examines contemporary issues that are driving change and is split into four chapters: Chapter 3 addresses the interdisciplinary nature of research involving children; Chapter 4 orients a research perspective around children's rights; the fifth chapter reflects on the complexities of the roles of researcher and researched and the sixth is devoted to the most recent development in this field - research led by children and young people. Part 3 is concerned with implications for policy and practice.

Throughout the book specific examples of research are drawn on to illustrate points made in the narrative discourse. These research examples are boxed and form a central part of the book. Readers are encouraged to engage in the activities which are linked to the research examples. Distributed across chapters are short 'pause for thought' moments which encapsulate particularly poignant or controversial statements that stimulate critical reflection. At strategic places, key points are drawn together to aid synthesis. Each chapter contains suggestions for further reading to encourage more in-depth engagement with some of the issues. A summary of content covered completes each chapter.

The book is mainly centred on the UK, although it does draw on some examples from around the world for comparative purposes and to underline the importance of adopting a global perspective and how much we can learn from child research in other countries.

2 The Issues and Debates Defined

Introduction and key questions

Before we can rethink our approach to children and research it is important to have an understanding of how children have featured in research over time. In the first part of this chapter, therefore, I present a historical overview and then move on to examine some of the contemporary issues and debates that are central to a reshaping of our thinking around children and research. This begins with an exploration of power dynamics and political influence and concludes with a look at some of the critical issues, in particular ethical considerations around informed consent and absence of harm.

- Can children ever just 'be' or are they always in a state of 'becoming'?
- Did a shift from research 'on' to research 'with' children affect power dynamics?
- How do politics affect research involving children?
- What is the difference between research on children, *about* children, *with* children and *by* children?
- What ethical considerations should inform research involving children?

Historical overview of children and research

> ## Can children ever just 'be' or are they always in a state of 'becoming'?

Children have not always been a focus of research in the way that physics or astronomy engaged the minds of scholars in the Renaissance period. Indeed until the twentieth century children did not have a recognized status, being viewed simply as 'adults in waiting' and therefore of little interest to the scholarly mind. The earliest focus on children came from seventeenth-century philosophers who initiated theoretical debate around the nature of childhood (Hendrick, 1997). Attitudes to children and childhood were largely shaped by religion and culture. The Puritan dogma of this era considered children to be innately evil, born with 'original sin' that must be purged from them. John Locke (1632–1704) was the first to challenge this, arguing that far from being innately pre-determined, children were a product of their environment, born as a 'blank slate' waiting for environmental influences to shape them. He was the first philosopher to acknowledge that children had specific needs of their own, needs that were different from adults, although these needs were still correlated to 'becoming' an adult rather than 'being' a child. In the next century Rousseau (1762) constructed childhood as a pure and idyllic time and this persisted into the nineteenth century when wealthy, middle class families embraced childhood as something to be protected and enjoyed. It was very different, of course, for working class families where children as young as five were put to work in factories and viewed as an economic commodity.

In the wake of the industrialization period and pressure from socialists, politicians were persuaded to legislate to put an end to child labour and replace it with education (1842 Mines Act; 1844 Factory Act; 1870 Education Act). Child-rearing was glorified as a mother's most important occupation. Actual research on children, as opposed to theoretical discourse about them, was born out of a new interest in child health and wellbeing. Many of the early documented research studies were observations on children's development. They focused on improving the health and welfare of children and enhancing their mental prowess. Large-scale quantitative studies used scientific methods from which generalizations could be drawn and universal laws established. This era of positivist research harvested many studies in areas of nutrition, health and preventive medicine such as childhood vaccinations. It had many positive benefits including a measurable fall in the rate of infant mortality.

Comparative studies of children's physical wellbeing and mortality rates also exposed inequalities among the different social class structures and heralded a new wave of research spearheaded by politicians and welfare reformers. The rise of the Welfare State brought with it an increasing interference in the child-rearing practices of the nation. Reformers tried to impose middle-class values on working class families, eschewing many of their more flexible, traditional practices in favour of rigid rules such as breast feeding on demand which took no account of mothers who needed to work. The numbers of Child Guidance Clinics grew rapidly and with it a new impetus for childhood research.

Urbanization brought together large numbers of children into concentrated areas compared to the scattered rural demographics of pre-industrialized times. Compulsory schooling (1880) facilitated easy access to cohorts of children and fuelled a growing interest in developmental psychology. Early developmental psychologists regarded the child as incomplete and malleable, developing differently in response to different stimuli. 'The child is portrayed, like the laboratory rat, as being at the mercy of external stimuli: passive and conforming' (James and Prout, 1997, 13). Childhood was divided into age-graded developmental stages. Children became the 'objects' of research. The researcher was depicted as the expert on children's lives: how children think, reason, communicate, even on the effects of aspects of children's personality and environment. Schools and nurseries provided ideal opportunities to observe large numbers of children of the same age at the same time under 'controlled' conditions. This made it possible to analyse average ability and arrive at standard definitions of what constituted 'normal'. One of the tools for establishing what was 'normal' was the intelligence test. Psychologists produced a range of different tests for measuring mental processes. This led to the 'labelling' of children and segregation according to their Intelligence Quotient (IQ). While research of this nature added to the body of knowledge about cognitive development, it also produced some negative outcomes particularly for those children who were assigned to 'mentally defective institutions' on the basis of their IQ scores. Furthermore, researchers such as Louis Terman (1877–1956), who regarded IQ as genetically and racially determined, opened the door to abusive practices of eugenic social control and the promotion of the image of the white child as superior.

One of the most famous child development researchers was Jean Piaget (1896–1980). His work outlined clearly defined stages of cognitive growth from the *sensory-motor* stage of infancy through *pre-conceptual, intuitive* and *concrete* to the *formal operations* of adolescence and adulthood. Movement from one stage to the next was argued to be dependent on achievement of a specific 'schema' of physical and mental actions and a gradual process of 'de-centring'. He maintained that all normally developing children pass through these stages and, if not at the same rate then certainly in the same sequence. A powerful critique of this kind of developmentalism was that it took no account of socio-cultural differences (Burman, 1994). This led to a new style of child research with an emphasis on the socially interactive nature of learning. Lev Vygotsky (1896–1934) was its most famous proponent. This social constructivist perspective, as it became known, eschews assumptions about social structures that define childhood. Within a socially constructed world there are no constraints and childhood is not viewed in any precise, identifiable form (James, Jenks and Prout, 1998).

A desire to understand other people's social processes led to the emergence of anthropological enquiry with its ethnographic style of research around the end of the nineteenth century. Classical ethnography entails researchers being immersed in fieldwork and living among the subjects of their research for an extended period. Margaret Mead (1901–1978) was among the first anthropologists to engage in research about children. Her ethnographic studies titled *Coming of Age in Samoa* (1928) and *Growing up in New Guinea* (1930) illuminated the lifestyles of Samoan and New Guinea children and young people. She wanted to explore whether nature or nurture determined adolescent behaviour, although her research methods were later criticized for using Western developmental theory as a reference norm. Anthropologists do not assume children have an individual sense of the self. Their ethnographic research demonstrates that in many parts of the world the greater collective of the family is prized above the rights of each individual and raises some interesting questions about the extent to which the child rights movement can be applied universally.

Key points

- In the early seventeenth century attitudes to children and childhood were largely shaped by religion and culture.
- John Locke (1632–1704) theorized that children were a product of their environment, born as a 'blank slate' waiting for environmental influences to shape them.
- In the eighteenth century childhood was seen as a time of innocence and purity.
- The end of child labour and the introduction of compulsory schooling (1870) heralded a new research interest in child health and wellbeing.
- Most of the twentieth century was dominated by scientific, laboratory-style enquiry. Developmental psychology research focused on norm-referenced cognition and linear stages of development.
- Research that led to IQ testing opened the door to abusive practices of eugenic social control and the promotion of the image of the white child as superior.
- Towards the end of the twentieth century thinking had moved on to embrace childhood as a socially constructed entity.

Activity

You might like to construct your own time line to show the major events in the history of child research.

Sociological research with children

All the research referred to thus far has been research 'on' children where children are the 'objects' of adult research. This persisted late into the twentieth century until sociologists began to question the 'assumed' roles and relationships in child research. It is only recently in what some are calling 'the new sociology of childhood' that interest in children as a distinct entity has grown. James, Jenks and Prout (1998) introduced the notion of 'presociological' and 'sociological' models of childhood.

Research example: models of childhood

The work of James, Jenks and Prout (1998) has been significant in influencing the direction of research with children. It broadened the childhood research arena beyond the constraints of developmentalism into the realms of agency. James (1999) illustrated this through the coining of four models of childhood. The first of these was the '*developing child*', a traditional model predicated on theories of developmental psychology in which the child moves from child to adult status in defined stages. Adult professionals use norms of competence, normality, deviation and pathology against which to measure child development and wellbeing (Woodhead and Faulkner, 2008). The researcher is depicted as the expert on every aspect of children's lives and enquiry is based on hypotheses, control groups and laboratory-style experiments.

The second of James' models is the '*tribal child*'. Unlike the 'developing child', this model assumes children are socially competent and autonomous within their own cultural worlds, an assertion of the integrity of the child perspective. This model uses qualitative, ethnographic-style methods that seek to highlight divisions between childhood and adulthood.

> [Children] were not to be labelled as '*pre*-operational' or '*pre*-moral' or *pre*-anything else. Children were just different. This perspective cast a new light on the question of children's linguistic competencies: what children meant was what they said and the ethnographer's job became simply one of translation and then interpretation. It did not matter that these meanings might not be congruent with those of the adult world. Any ambiguity was welcomed as an illustration of the child's perspective on the world, a completely different point of view. (James, 1999, 239)

James' third model is the '*adult child*'. The status of the child in this model is a player inhabiting a shared adult–child world. The focus is on children's perspectives of the adult world they are obliged to inhabit rather than children's observations of their child peers. Adult and child actions are still delineated on age and gender lines with the child being perceived as less important than the adult.

James' fourth model is the '*social child*'. This model is based on the notion of childhood as a transient stage in life during which children engage in everyday activities as social actors in their own right. Research approaches adopt data-collection methods which privilege this and use mediums that are part of children's everyday experience such as drawing, painting, singing or telling a story. Children's competencies are accepted as different rather than inferior. They have a unique identity as social actors in ever-changing social and cultural contexts.

This widening of the scope of childhood to a societal level spawned an interest in research that gives voice to an agenda of children's rights and to an increased focus on childhood as a social category and children as a distinct population group. This led to developments about the ways in which children should be involved in research with a growing recognition of the value of ethnography and a resulting convergence between sociology and anthropology in the grounded study of childhood. The rights-based perspective prompted expectations that children should be active participants. Research 'with' rather than research 'on' children became a dominant discourse.

Activity

Think about the different stages of child research depicted in the historical overview and in James' four representations of the child. How do you think these changes have been reflected in research methods adopted with children?

Power dynamics in research involving children

Did a shift from research 'on' to research 'with' children affect power dynamics?

Power relations between adults and children are inextricably linked to cultural practices. In Western countries this is heavily influenced by generational ordering (Alanen, 1992) and competency barriers (Woodhead and Faulkner, 2008). Children are largely confined to the private spaces of home and family and kept away from the public arenas of policy and decision-making. School, while it is a less private space than the home, is one of the most governed childhood environments outside custodial institutions. Children, as a powerless minority group struggle to have their voices heard or their views acted upon. These power dynamics are also very evident in research involving children. It is adults who control the research agendas, formulate the questions, design the methods and interpret the findings. Children might play a small part in this as participants or co-researchers – commonly at the data-collection stage – but are rarely involved in the analysis of their data. This is overlain with a perception that children's participation in research is a gift in the power of adults to bestow rather than a child's fundamental right (Hamill and Boyd, 2002). Historically, Western children have been silenced either through oppressive conventions that prize children being 'seen and not heard' or by their voice being distorted in the mediated accounts created by historians, anthropologists, sociologists and psychologists (Lloyd-Smith and Tarr, 2000). Nor is it easy for children, without any 'authorial voice' (Hendrick, 2000), to challenge adult research accounts.

The contention that adults have power over children is indisputable and has a significant bearing on the control they exercise over how children's views are accessed and therefore on how research about children is conducted and received. The power of adult views always take precedence over children's views and confines children to subordinate roles in their societies (Taylor, 2000).

Activity

In 2002 the Scottish Parliament was considering legislation to prohibit the smacking of children. Research into the views of children on smacking found that over 90 per cent of those who took part were opposed to smacking (Scottish Executive, 2002). However consultation processes with adults in Scotland found that, in the main, they were opposed to a ban. The adults' views prevailed and the proposal was subsequently dropped in 2003.

Take a little time to think about rhetoric and reality in power relations between adults and children that this example raises? Rhetoric is pointing to contemporary child research being repositioned to articulate a rights perspective. The example here suggests that, in reality, this can only happen when it suits adult agendas. Can you think of any similar examples of your own?

Power is not just about force but also about the creation of knowledge which renders children doubly disempowered. As has already been shown, children's knowledge can be disregarded and they can still be controlled by force, however benevolently that force may be constructed by adults. Age and competency are frequently used as delineating factors in power relations between adults and children and an obstacle to their full participation in research. The competency debates are a legacy from the dominant period of developmental psychology and have been robustly challenged (Christensen and Prout, 2002; Woodhead and Faulkner, 2008). Equally, age barriers are being torn down by approaches such as Clark and Moss's (2001) 'mosaic' technique where very young children actively participate in data collection. A further factor that sustains unequal adult–child power relations is a belief that adults have superior knowledge. Undoubtedly this is the case in some areas of life but with regard to childhood – in the sense of what it is like to be a child – then it is children who have the superior knowledge, as Mayall (2000, 122) states,

> I want to acquire from them [children] their own unique knowledge and assessment of what it means to be a child; for though I can remember some things about being a child, I may have forgotten much, and childhoods may vary and have probably changed over the years since I was a child.

Location and context are central tenets of power relations in child research. The school environment is a prime example of this.

Activity

Citizenship is a compulsory curriculum subject for some ages of pupils in England and Wales. Current discourses about citizenship emphasize the recognition of difference and giving voice to those currently excluded. The concept of participation is central to any definition of citizenship (Devine, 2002). For children to have a voice and identify themselves as citizens, there has to be acknowledgement of their status as social actors in their own right. Yet, ironically, the school environment lends little credence to the actuality of child citizenship status. For example children were not able to voice their protest against the 2003 Gulf War without fear of truant labelling and threats of prosecution. While women in the workplace are successfully challenging oppressive dress codes on a platform of human rights, girls are still struggling, in some schools, to overturn prejudice about the wearing of trousers. At a time when European directives are advising on maximum weekly employment hours for the working population, children have little power to challenge the school hours and homework hours that are arbitrarily set by educationalists.

Where do you think children feature in the citizenship debate? Can children ever be equal in terms of citizenship? Can research about citizenship influence policy change? If so, what kind of research is needed?

Some writers (e.g. Morrow and Richards, 1996) have questioned the ethics of research where children are 'captive subjects'. In schools, adults control children's use of time, occupation of space, choice of clothing, times of eating – even their mode of social interaction. The UNCRC (1989) article 31 relates to the right of the child to rest and leisure and to engage in play and yet there appears to be an expectation that these entitlements do not relate to anything that happens in school hours.

Pause for thought

In Latin the word 'ludus' has a twin meaning of both 'schooling' and 'entertainment' and Plato advised parents that play was a good preparation for citizenship. In Ancient Greece, education and enjoyment were seen as overlapping entities that shaped young people's lives (Lazos, 2002, cited in Hartas, 2008). Indeed, the terms 'education' and 'youth' had a common root in the Greek language.

Another consideration is the power exerted in terms of influence with regard to hierarchies of what is important to study at school. Subjects that are valued as core learning such as maths, language and science dominate the timetable in comparison to marginalized subjects like art, music and PE and convey implicit messages about their relative merits. Children are not consulted about the weighting of subjects in the timetable despite evidence (see Pollard and Triggs, 2000) that they find certain subjects more appealing. Neither are they consulted about the distribution of work/play time. The absence of children's voice in decisions about the organization of their time and space in school works against the concept of children as social actors with the right to a voice. Moreover, it undermines the requirement of the 2002 Education Act for schools to consult the views of pupils.

> School and schooling is experienced as something 'done to' the children, legitimized by a discourse which prioritizes adult/future-oriented needs and expectations over present lived experience. The emphasis lies with the preparation of children as future citizens, equipped with the skills (productivity, competitiveness, comportment and control) to contribute as adults to the needs of modern industrial/postindustrial society. (Devine, 2002, 312)

Further legislation was introduced in 2008 which places a duty on all maintained schools in England Wales to consider the views of pupils in matters that affected school experience.

Activity

Legal age delineators that control children's lives are not always reflected in children's real world experiences. For example:

- In the UK children are legal minors until the age of 18 – yet many enter the workforce, drive a car and join the armed forces while they are still legally 'children'.
- The legal age of sexual consent is 16 – yet many children are sexually active at 14 and some younger. Many under 16s also receive contraception without their parents' consent.
- The legal age of criminal responsibility is 10 – so a child of 10 could be criminally liable for assault if he or she smacks another individual but a parent can lawfully smack a 10-year-old. 10-year-olds have no power commensurate with their age of criminal responsibility, they have no powers of consent, no authority over others and no legal decision-making rights.

Can you think of other examples? Think about how research involving children could bring about change. What kind of studies would you recommend? How would you disseminate findings so that they had an impact?

How do politics affect research involving children?

Some reference to political governance has already been alluded to earlier in the chapter with the plethora of child development research that was politically linked to health, wellbeing and intellectual competency in the mid-twentieth century. Similar issues feature just as prominently in contemporary politics. The focus, however, has shifted towards a children's rights agenda, spearheaded by the United Nations Convention on the Rights of the Child (UNCRC) (1989) which all countries other than Somalia and the United States signed up to. This charter was a catalyst for change, demanding its membership ensure that children are listened to and consulted on all matters affecting their lives and their views given due weight (Articles 12 and 13). Furthermore, it upheld the right of children to high standards of research about their lives (Article 3). The politics of research involving children is inextricably linked to the discourse on children's voice which Thorne (2002, 251) sees as 'a metaphor for political recognition, self-determination and full presence in knowledge, it is the right to speak *and* to be listened to'. A new wave of participatory research was born which purported to consult and listen to children by involving them more directly in the research process. This commitment to research 'with' children as opposed to research 'on' children was patchily implemented. Governments interpreted the Convention's mandate liberally – and some would argue, cynically – especially references in Article 12 of the UNCRC to children's age and competence.

> States Parties shall assure to the child *who is capable of forming his or her own views* the right to express those views freely in all matters affecting the child, the views of the child being given due weight *in accordance with the age and maturity of the child.* (italic text is my emphasis)

In the case of the UK, the Government delayed bringing in legislation to embed the principles of the UNCRC until 15 years later. The Government was able to retreat behind adult constructs of what constituted age and maturity and the point at which a child was deemed capable of forming his or her own view, claiming that the requirements of the UNCRC were already covered in the 1989 Children Act. In response to criticism at the United Nations Special Summit on Children's Rights (2002), the UK Government finally took action. This resulted in the formulation of the *Every Child Matters* Green Paper (DfES [Department for Education and Skills], 2003) which identified five outcomes important for children to lead happy lives – 'being healthy'; 'staying safe'; 'enjoying and achieving'; 'making a positive contribution' and 'achieving economic well-being'. This was followed into legislation with the 2004 Children's Act.

Activity

- Being healthy
- Staying safe
- Enjoying and achieving
- Making a positive contribution
- Achieving economic well-being

What do you think about these five outcomes for children to lead happy lives arrived at in the *Every Chid Matters* Green Paper? Do you have a view about the linking of enjoyment with achievement in the third outcome? Would you have come up with different outcomes? Do you think children would have come up with different outcomes? How much do you think they were consulted?

What is the difference between research *on* children, *about* children, *with* children and *by* children?

The *Every Child Matters* agenda initiated a wave of participatory research in which children sat on advisory panels and were involved in collecting data alongside adult researchers. Children were able to play a bigger role in decision-making processes affecting their lives. Indeed, governments now *required* children's services and organizations to include child consultations in their policy and practice. This set the stage for a final empowerment push and the positioning of children as researchers in their own right (see Kellett 2005; 2005a). Instead of research *on* children as we saw in early developmental psychology experiments, or research *about* children in explorations of socially constructed childhoods, or research *with* children in the participatory agendas driven by *Every Child Matters*, came the prospect of research *by* children. Research *by* children goes a step further than children as participant or co-researchers. Children are empowered to lead their own research, set their own agendas, decide the topics that are important to research, choose the methods to employ and actively engage in analysis and dissemination of their own findings. Child–child research is characteristically different from adult–child research and generates different data. Children are party to the subculture of childhood which gives them an insider perspective that adults cannot access and thus have the potential to create a valuable new body of knowledge about childhoods and children's lived experiences. This concept is discussed in depth in Chapter 6, so I will not elaborate any further at this point.

Key points

- In Western countries, adult–child power relations are heavily influenced by generational ordering and competency barriers.
- Children are experts on their own lives but power-dynamics get in the way of their voices being heard.
- Legal age delineators that control children's lives are not always reflected in children's real world experiences. Research can be an agent of change.
- Research involving children can be expressed as four typologies: research *on* children; research *about* children; research *with* children; and research *by* children.

Critical ethical issues

The next section of the chapter moves to consider some of the critical ethical issues bound up in research involving children. There are three topics of focus: informed consent, confidentiality and the safeguarding of research participants from harm.

Informed consent

Until quite recently children were not consulted about being part of a research project. At best, their legal guardian would be approached to give consent, at worst the research would be carried out in captive environments, such as schools, where researchers sought blanket consent from a headteacher without reference to the children concerned. How often have children turned up to a class to find a researcher sitting in a corner with a notepad, watching their every move and scribbling furiously? Did anyone ever ask the children if they objected to this outsider observing them? This situation is beginning to change and ethical researchers will ensure that they seek consent from children as well as their legal guardians before embarking on any research activity. Some data-collection activities lend themselves more readily to consent by children than others. Interviews probably rank highest and child protection concerns have made it increasingly difficult for researchers to do one-to-one interviews with children without very rigorous consent practices and criminal records bureau checks. Nevertheless group interviews are still open to exploitation. The 'safety in numbers' aspect sometimes results in group interviews being set up in schools without appropriate consents. This brings us to a consideration of what constitutes appropriate consent.

Before individuals can give their consent they need some understanding of what is involved and exactly what they are consenting to. This is what we call informed consent. Asking children to give consent on the basis of a brief statement such as 'I'm doing some research on children and television' is not sufficient information on which they can make an informed consent decision. Exactly what kind of research about children and television? Will it involve any experiments? Will participants be interviewed, if so will this be alone or in a group? Will their contribution be confidential? What is the researcher trying to find out? Who will see the findings? Where will they be reported? These are the kinds of questions that need to be answered in order to make an informed choice about participation.

Activity

Indra is talking to a group of 13-year-old girls at a youth Centre.

My name is Indra and I'm a researcher employed by Plumpton Primary Care Trust. I'm doing some research on girls' experiences of sex education. Would you be willing to be interviewed?

Is this enough information for the girls to make an informed decision about whether to participate in the interviews? If not, think about what else they might need to know?

The issue of informed consent with regard to participating children is complex because of their minority status. Informed consent is additionally required from those who have legal care and control – a parent, guardian or local authority. Sometimes there can be a conflict of interest. Children may wish to participate in a study but parents refuse consent. In most cases, parental wishes take precedence but there are some exceptions, especially where older children are concerned. Legally, a child is a minor until the age of 18, but some rights are obtained at 16. Some famous legal precedents have been set where young people have won the right to overturn legal guardians' wishes. A famous example is the Gillick case. (Gillick v. W. Norfolk and Wisbech, 1985) in which the House of Lords upheld the view that a 14-year-old child who had sufficient understanding of her situation could consent to medical treatment and that her parents/guardians did not have the right to override the child's decision.

Debate continues about the age at which children are deemed responsible enough to give their informed consent. We specify 7 as the 'age of reason' and 10 as the age of criminal responsibility (in the UK) but we do not specify an age for informed consent. My own opinion is that informed consent is a fundamental right of every child irrespective of age or ability. There is an obligation on the part of the researcher to explain in language the child can understand, what his or her research study is about including any risks or problems associated with the study along with a brief summary of the methods and a time plan. This can be done through child-friendly information leaflets, drawings, verbal explanations and scenario-enacting activities designed to help children understand what the research is about and what they are agreeing to.

Activity

Here is an example of Indra talking to a 6-year-old boy about being interviewed for her research project about children's fears at school.

- You only need to talk to me if you want to and you can change your mind at any time.
- No-one can make you talk to me, it is just up to you and no-one will be cross or disappointed if you decide not to talk to me.
- You don't have to answer all my questions just the ones you want to.
- You can stop talking to me whenever you want or have a break whenever you want.
- To help you decide it might be a good idea to talk it over with a friend or a parent.
- If you agree I'll make a tape of our talk but will keep this locked in a safe place so that no-one else can listen to it.
- I'll let you listen to the tape and you can tell me if you want to change anything.
- I won't talk to anyone about what you say, unless you tell me there is a possibility of someone being harmed.
- If you give me permission to use any of what you tell me in my research report I'll change your name so that other people won't know it was you who said this.

Do you think Indra has given enough information to this 6-year-old boy in language he can understand? Can he make an *informed* decision about participating? Is there anything else you would say to him?

Informed consent that is ethically obtained does not involve any element of coercion or inducement on the part of the researcher. This is particularly important in contexts where participants are relatively powerless – e.g. children in schools or young offender institutions. Nor does the consent process stop here. We also have to consider the issue of *ongoing consent*. Participants need to understand that they can withdraw their consent at any time and for any reason. It is helpful to think in terms of a hierarchy of consent with 'proxy' consent at the bottom and ongoing consent at the top.

informed and ongoing consent – a child consents with understanding of the full implications of the research and continues to give consent through the lifetime of the research

informed consent – a child consents with understanding of the full implications of the research

assent – a child acquiesces without knowledge or understanding
proxy consent – a third party such as a teacher or health worker consents on the child's behalf.

Pause for thought

What about children with learning difficulties? A helpful initiative I devised when doing some research with children who had severe and complex learning difficulties to ensure they were comfortable about participating in my research was something I called a 'circle of consent' (Kellett, 2001). A circle of consent places a child with learning difficulties at the centre of a virtual circle and surrounds him with individuals who know him well, can understand and interpret his needs and have his best interests at heart. A circle might consist of a class friend, a sibling, a support worker, a teacher, a parent, etc. Collectively these individuals take responsibility for informed consent by observing participation sessions and preventing any activity which might occasion him distress or discomfort.

Key points

- Children – and their legal guardians – need sufficient information about a research project to make an informed consent decision.
- Researchers should seek consent from children additionally to any given by their legal guardians.
- Children must be free to be able to dissent without fear of reprisals.
- Consent can be withdrawn at any time and for any reason.
- Researchers must consider *ongoing* consent.

Confidentiality and anonymity

We have an ethical duty to protect participants from public scrutiny. Wherever possible researchers assure participants that the data they collect will be treated confidentially and their anonymity preserved. Children should be afforded the same rights as adults in this respect. Children are commonly anxious about anything they say in an interview being conveyed back to their teachers or parents. Confidentiality is something that researchers should be able to guarantee with one notable exception – that of disclosures about abuse or harm. It is expected that names will be changed when a study is reported but sometimes the population sample is so small and/or the location of the research so conspicuous that total anonymity cannot be guaranteed and researchers need to be honest with participants about this. Special care has to be taken with video and photographic data because these are more difficult to anonymize. Data ought to be destroyed once all the analysis is complete but many researchers are reluctant to destroy data, clinging to a 'just in case' rationale and keeping their data for years, sometimes decades, beyond its shelf life.

Pause for thought

Sometimes research video data of children get into the public domain – initially with full consent of children's legal guardians. Consider a programme such as *Child of Our Time*. This is a research documentary charting the social development of a group of children over a longitudinal period. It is broadcast on a BBC channel and could be video-taped and saved by any viewer. Some of the footage shows children having temper tantrums and other actions they may find embarrassing in their teenage years. The children were too young to give their consent to being filmed when they were toddlers and even if they exercised a right to withdraw ongoing consent at an older age, it would be impossible to track down and destroy all the copies of the film data which might have been made. How can a child's ongoing consent be honoured in such circumstances?

Interview with Carmel Smith about research with children

Carmel Smith *is Lecturer at Carlow College, Ireland, and has over twenty years' experience of direct work with children in a wide range of practice settings.*

Mary: You have done a lot of research with children involving interviews. What do you think are the main issues related to confidentiality?

Carmel: I think the first major issue is that many children have no experience, and few expectations, of confidentiality from adults. Parents talk about their children to each other or to other family members or to friends. Teachers talk to parents or other teachers, social workers talk to an array of other professionals and so on. In fact, not treating children confidentially is seen by most professionals as a way of both protecting and controlling children and young people. Consequently, the people that children look to, and expect confidentiality from, in their everyday lives tend to be either siblings or friends – in other words, other children and young people. This is particularly the case in teenage years when the young person's peer group and close friends generally become increasingly important. Children's expectations of confidentiality in these relationships are closely associated with unconditional loyalty. Therefore, an adult offering to speak confidentially with a child or young person may well present a new or unusual scenario and one that needs to be carefully facilitated by the researcher.

In reality of course, there can never be a promise of absolute confidentiality in a research interview whether it is with a child or an adult. There is always the possibility that the researcher might have to breach confidentiality in extreme circumstances. The challenges around confidentiality therefore, are not posed by the tiny minority of obvious cases requiring intervention but by those occupying the vast middle ground and the extent to which the researcher is able to contain their own anxiety. Trusting that the child or young person will tell us what they want to tell us, and won't tell us what they don't want us to know, allows the researcher to 'let go' in the research arena and leave the space for the child to lead and to tell their own story in their own way and at their own pace.

Mary: What kind of confidentiality issues worry children? Can you give me any examples?

Carmel: Children frequently worry about confidentiality in terms of interview content because they do not want to upset adults whom they care about or they do not want to get themselves or others into trouble. This was something that arose in a study I undertook with adopted children, some of whom spoke of wondering about their birth mother on a regular basis yet not feeling able to mention this to their much loved adoptive parents for fear of causing them distress. This is a reflection of children's everyday lives when they frequently do not share their worries with adults for a number of reasons. For example, if a child is being bullied at school the child might feel that it is their own fault, they might not want to worry their parent or they might be scared about their parent's reaction. Children may also be aware that telling an adult, such as a teacher, is equivalent to relinquishing their power to that adult who can choose to act on their behalf, or 'for their own good', regardless of what the child thinks or wants. My experience is that children often know more, and have a far greater range of feelings, than adults around them realise. They believe that adults will feel happier if they think children are unaware of certain things and children may safeguard their knowledge accordingly. The issue of confidentiality in research is therefore intertwined with the issue of trust in the relationship between the child and the researcher.

Confidentiality is of course closely tied to access in terms of research with children and access is usually gained via gatekeepers. I have found that children tend to focus on more immediate questions about confidentiality such as who will listen to the tape, whether parents will be allowed to read the interview transcripts and when and how the tape will be destroyed. Parents tend to be the ones who consider the wider implications of the research, for example asking about avenues of redress if they want to make a complaint either during or after a study has been completed.

Mary: We make a lot of claims about anonymity but some children actually want you to use their real names. How would you manage this kind of situation?

Carmel: Again, I would not necessarily make any huge distinction between children and adults. My first consideration would be whether using real names places the child at any risk –physical or psychological – either now or in the future and whether the child has thought through the possible implications. For example, telling their story to an interviewer in a one-to-one interview, and perhaps seeing it in its entirety in transcript form, is very different from seeing an edited version in a book or a selection of random quotations in a journal article. My second consideration would be whether identifying the child would also enable others to be identified which would, of course, be unacceptable. I would perhaps explore with the child whether using a meaningful name (perhaps their middle name or the name of a favourite toy) would suffice. If the child still felt strongly about the issue I would ask an independent adult, such as a colleague, to think through the ethical issues with me before granting the child's wish. My actual experience has been the opposite. I have had parents wanting to be very open about their children's participation in a research project whereas I was less certain that it was what the children wanted. This presented an interesting piece of negotiation with the gatekeepers on behalf of the two children involved!

Absence of harm

The *Child of Our Time* example mentioned above raises an important issue about the potential for causing harm during research activity. It is vital that any research process whether this involves children as participants or as researchers in their own right does not cause harm. Harm can be physical, mental or emotional. It would be easy to recognize if a research process was causing physical harm and most human beings would outlaw any such practice. It is not as easy to identify potential mental and/or emotional harm. Examples of emotional harm as a consequence of engagement in research could be anxiety, embarrassment, depression, mistrust, or loss of self-esteem. For example, interviewing children about their bullying experiences might result in feelings of anxiety or depression being stirred up. Carrying out public tests on children to research their memory recall abilities might result in a loss of self-esteem. Research methods that make children look foolish might lead to embarrassment. These are all sources of potential harm.

Activity

Gerard and Paavan are two boys who are keen on – and very good at – running. They are interested in doing some research about sport and about running in particular. They would like to investigate if there is any correlation between height, weight and speed of running. Their research design includes taking height and weight measurements from all their class mates during a maths lesson, then requiring the same children to run a timed 100 metre distance during a PE lesson.

Do you think this is an ethical research project? What potential harm(s) might be caused? How could they modify the research design in a more ethical way? Do you think the topic itself is too sensitive to be researched?

Sometimes there is a tension between potential harm to an individual and potential good to a greater number and these situations require careful reflection and fine judgement.

Research example: the Bobo doll experiment

The Bobo doll experiment was conducted by a researcher called Albert Bandura in 1961. He was studying patterns of behaviour associated with aggression and wanted to find out if young children imitate aggression if it is modelled by others. If you want to read the original study, it was reported by Bandura and his colleagues Dorothea and Sheila Ross in an article entitled 'Transmission of aggression through imitation of aggressive models' (1961) in *Journal of Abnormal and Social Psychology*, 63, 575–582.

There have been many replications and adaptations of Bandura's experiment but the essence of it is as follows: A child is taken into a room full of toys, one of which is a Bobo doll (a Bobo doll is a blow-up doll about the size of a small child with a weighted base so that it cannot fall over, if knocked it simply bounces back into position). After a little while an adult enters the toy room and starts to be aggressive towards the Bobo doll, hitting it with a mallet and verbally abusing it. The adult leaves the room and the researcher waits to see if the child will imitate the violence towards the Bobo doll or continue to play with other toys in a non-aggressive way. The experiment was repeated in the television series *Child of Our Time* with a small girl of around 3 or 4 years old. The little girl, who was looking very anxious when the adult was hitting the Bobo doll waits for a little while and then approaches the Bobo doll. In a small voice and with a tiny fist she starts to hit the doll in the face, at first tentatively and then more vigorously, censoring it for being naughty.

This research graphically illustrates the hypothesis that children imitate others' violence. While these findings inform our understanding, the cost of generating this knowledge are considerable. What harm might be done by an experiment like this?

Ethics committees can be helpful when trying to untangle all the ethical nuances that have to be considered in the design of a research project. Most organizations undertaking research have access to an ethics committee which advise, and ultimately police, ethical practice. With the growing number of research projects being carried out by child researchers some serious thought must now be given to specialist ethics committees being formed in schools and other children's organizations to support them.

Summary

This chapter has:
- Presented a historical overview of children and research.
- Looked at the differences between research *on* children, *about* children, *with* children and *by* children.
- Explored how power dynamics affect the way research involving children has evolved and how these influence research relationships.

- Examined political influences in research involving children and how these have informed debates on competency, citizenship, participation and voice.
- Considered the critical ethical issues of informed consent, confidentiality, anonymity and absence of harm.

Suggested further reading

Alderson, P. and Morrow, V. (2004) *Ethics, Social Research and Consulting with Children and Young People* (2nd edn), Ilford: Barnado's.

A comprehensive and challenging coverage of a range of ethical considerations in research involving children.

Cunningham, H. (2006) *The Invention of Childhood*, London: BBC Books.

A complete chronological history of childhood in Britain over the last 1,000 years.

Hallett, C. and Prout, A. (2003) (eds) *Hearing the Voices of Children: Social Policy for a New Century*, London and New York: Routledge Falmer.

Makes an important contribution to debates around increased participation for children and young people and offers a new perspective on listening to children. The editors lay down a challenge to convert the rhetoric on participation into real practice for the twenty-first century and address critical issues which need to be resolved.

Farrell, A. (2005) (ed.) *Ethical Research with Children*, Maidenhead: Open University Press.

Features coverage of ethical research with marginalized groups of children relating to indigenous populations, young children (under 3) and children with disabilities.

Part 2
Contemporary Issues

Interdisciplinary Research Involving Children 3

Chapter Outline

Introduction and key questions

This chapter examines the growing interdisciplinary nature of research involving children. As the status of children in society shifts, so an interest in childhoods and children's lives has extended across new disciplines. High profile child protection cases, the rise of child poverty and concerns about child labour have kept a sharp focus on children. All of those working with children whether as practitioners or academics are seeing the value of exploring childhoods from multiple perspectives. Sharing of knowledge only enhances our understanding of children's worlds. Good communication is the key: communication between and across disciplines and within multi-agency service settings. Research within an interdisciplinary context is revealing difficulties as well as opportunities. The politics of childhood and the position of children regarding the origins and nature of research about their lives are driving some of that interdisciplinarity.

- How interdisciplinary is research involving children becoming?
- What can we learn from a global focus to child research?
- Do different disciplines have different approaches to child research and is this a good or a bad thing?
- What are the challenges and tensions in multi-agency working?
- Can I be your research partner? The role of children as co-researchers in interdisciplinary child research.

How interdisciplinary is research involving children becoming?

As discussed in Chapter 2, research about children traditionally began in the scientific, psychological and medical domains of health, development and cognition where children were very much 'objects' of study. Research was pertinent to particular domains and while outcomes were accessible to the different domains there was little sharing of methods or perspectives. Contemporary approaches to child research are very different and the generation and application of knowledge is a more shared endeavour. In academic terms, 'interdisciplinary' means that distinct disciplines such as sociology, education, psychology, anthropology, etc. share their methods and perspectives in a combined approach to a child research topic for example child poverty. In professional practice terms, interdisciplinary refers to a similar shared approach to something, such as a specific childhood issue, would no longer be the sole domain of health professionals. Teachers, psychologists and other childhood professionals would contribute their various expertise. Multi-agency is a term that refers to another shared approach but from an organizational standpoint. For example a health centre, a police force, a school, a youth centre, a Connexions service and a Sure Start centre might all be liaising together to providing services for certain children.

The growth of Childhood Studies as an academic discipline and the embracing of children's rights as an expanding branch of legal studies has shifted perspectives towards a focus on agency and human rights and extended childhood research into other fields, notably sociology, cultural studies, anthropology, social policy, applied education, the law and economics (particularly, child labour) with an increasingly interdisciplinary – and global – range. This has created challenge for orthodox disciplines and emerging discourses of childhood give rise to tensions in collaborative relationships between disciplines.

The United Nations Convention on the Rights of the Child was the watershed that steered these foci towards children's rights, towards the nature and quality of childhoods and children's lived experiences. Sociological approaches epitomize this in being concerned with power relations in society and in questioning the taken for granted ways in which roles and relationships within societies are understood, including how we construct childhoods. In accepting the notion of children as co-constructors of society we are accepting that childhood is a permanent part of this social structure which invites empirical enquiry into how childhood relates to wider social forces (Christensen and Prout, 2005). It also broadens the study of childhood through comparative research. Christensen and Prout (2005, 51) make a salient point that when children are compared to other groups – e.g. the elderly – other social and economic arguments become apparent.

> It is well known, for example, that child poverty in the UK rose sharply in the 1980s and 1990s. Children as a group, however, saw a disproportionate rise in poverty compared to the rest of the population; in effect, as a group, they moved down the income distribution . . . poverty among children in the UK rose sharply at a time when it remained more or less stable in most other similar countries. This suggests that, unlike these other countries, the UK did not protect children against worsening economic conditions through welfare and social policy measures.

When child research draws on several disciplines to illuminate an aspect of children's lives it introduces an additional critical dimension because the different disciplines evaluate and question in different ways and this serves to highlight any tensions or flaws (as Christensen and Prout state in their quote about child poverty incidence) and this can only benefit children.

Child research has also mushroomed in Non Governmental Organizations (NGOs) because NGOs have been very proactive in embracing children's rights as a platform for research. Alongside this we have policy research about children's lives directly commissioned by governments and based on varying levels of consultation and/or participation of children. All of this results in a rich body of interdisciplinary, multi-disciplinary and politically-driven research underpinned by a diverse array of methods. It is not possible to cover all of this in one chapter and the suggested further reading will enable readers to follow up particular areas of interest in more depth. The aim of this chapter is to illustrate interdisciplinarity and changing research perspectives through a series of research examples and show how this is affecting outcomes for children.

Key points

- Childhood is a permanent part of our social structure and as such attracts research enquiry in its own right.
- A focus on children's agency and human rights has contributed to the growth of interdisciplinary child research.
- Academic interdisciplinarity relates to a sharing of methods and perspectives from distinct disciplines. Professional interdisciplinarity relates to a pooling of professional practice expertise. Multi-agency working relates to a joined-up approach from separate child service organizations.
- An interdisciplinary approach brings advantages but also some tensions and difficulties.

The rest of the chapter focuses on particular examples from academic interdisciplinarity, interdisciplinary professional practice and multi-agency working, drawing on some global perspectives.

What can we learn from a global focus to child research?

In the next research example I look at what we can learn from some research carried out in Tanzania where 50 per cent of the population are under the age of 18. This makes the subject of childhood and children's lives extremely important and enhances the poignancy of any research undertaken. Not surprisingly, the government has a particular interest in children's views about their lived experiences as this can inform how best to provide for them.

Research example: views of the children study, Tanzania

The full report 'Tanzanian Children's Perceptions of Education and Their Role in Society. Views of the Children 2007' can be obtained at

www.repoa.or.tz/documents_storage/ResearchandAnalysis/Views_of_the_Children_2007.pdf [accessed 04/02/09]

In 2007 the Tanzanian government commissioned a major survey of people's views as part of the poverty monitoring system of their National Strategy for Growth and Poverty Reduction. Children were an important part of this. The government recognized that eliciting the views of children needed a different approach from adults and therefore entered into a partnership with the NGO, Research on Poverty Alleviation (REPOA) – which has a thriving children's research programme and makes use of innovative qualitative and quantitative methods – to carry out the study. They in turn enlisted the support of the Research and Analysis Working Group (a sub-division of the Ministry of Planning, Economy and Empowerment) to help develop a research tool. Crucially, a children's workshop was set up to advise on the kinds of topics and questions that should be prioritized. Children were 'surveyed' using non-written, mixed methods. Quantitative questions were asked verbally, qualitative questions were framed through role playing scenarios and nuance of opinion was captured by drawing opinion lines on the ground and getting children to indicate where they would place themselves on such continuum lines. For example one question about teachers put a definition of kind, listening teachers at one end and strict, disciplinarian teachers at the other end of the line. In all, 500 children aged 7–14 from ten different regions were surveyed. Primary schools were used as the access point since many Tanzanian children only attend primary school (even though schooling is compulsory at secondary level) to get basic education before the economic demands of their families become too pressing. Once they stop attending school they dissipate into remote areas and are hard to reach. Below is an extract from the part of the report which summarizes the specific insights from the study (2007, 72–73).

a. Children understand the importance of the environment, both within the narrow confines of 'the teaching/learning environment', and within the broader issues of the environment around the school, tree planting and so on.

b. Their schooling teaches them the importance of good health, nutrition and clean water and yet in practice schools do minimal amounts to provide these amenities.

c. Learning is heavily reliant on notes from the blackboard and textbooks, and while the latter are liked, and in some schools quantities are improving, the lack of sufficient textbooks is still a source of frustration because there are just too few of them. Children are sharing books between very large numbers in class and are frustrated by not being able to read them in their own time.

d. With regard to teachers, there are some examples of excellent practice and dedication, such as efforts to fully integrate partially sighted children, and more generally indications that some teachers in some places are really making an effort to teach well. Students are very clear in what they want as a teacher: someone who really wants to teach, likes pupils, makes an effort, and in some cases that is what they are getting.

e. On the other hand, many teachers are apparently failing to meet basic contractual obligations. Failing to attend lessons comes across as a significant issue. Poor professional standards are being shown to children, such as in giving children notes but not actually explaining them. Corporal punishment regulations do not seem to be adhered to.

f. The overall picture is of schooling being quite a limited closed exercise with teachers explaining a fixed body of knowledge to a largely passive body of children. Communication between the school and parents in the upbringing of the children is weak.

g. Contributions in cash and kind are being expected in schools and children are being excluded from school because of non-payment.

h. The picture of whether things are getting better or worse since last year is mixed, with children having a wide variety of opinions. The vast majority of children feel that the best way to improve education is by more supply of side inputs, including infrastructure, teachers, school supplies, also better teachers, a more diverse curriculum, and other services in school (such as health). Children in Dar es Salaam were assertive in saying that increasing their own work and listening to teachers and parents would also be a factor.

Reflections on the research

Activity 1
Look closely at the findings documented in points a–h. What picture are you getting of the children's experiences? Can you separate out the positives and the negatives? Do you think the recommendations of the children will solve some of the problems, if not what issues are getting in the way?

Activity 2
Compare the main findings from the Tanzanian study with what you might expect such a survey in the UK to have revealed. Reflect on what we can learn from research undertaken in majority world countries and why it is important that child research should have a global focus.

Pause for thought

The adults who finalized the research tool separated the survey into two distinct halves, one that explored the views of children about their education and schooling and one that explored their views about society. Interestingly, one of the findings of the report was that the children themselves did not see these as separate entities. This suggests that, although children were involved in advising and shaping the questions and topics before the survey was undertaken, they were operating within an adult pre-conceived framework over which they were not consulted. Would the survey have generated additional/different data if children had been involved earlier in the planning processes?

Do different disciplines have different approaches to child research and is this a good or a bad thing?

Attempting to answer this question I find myself asking what is the purpose of research about children and childhoods? The answer comes very readily, it is to further our understanding of these phenomena in order to make childhoods better for children. If this is the starting premise then any research, from any discipline, that adds to our knowledge and understanding has a part to play. The exception is of course any discredited or unethical research. It is important to note that while there are many disciplines which undertake child research there are just as many disciplines which adopt interdisciplinary and multidisciplinary approaches. There are times when quantitative data are essential such as needing to know how many children are excluded from school or how many children are living in poverty and we can only obtain this information through large-scale survey-like data. However, the shift in recent decades has been to complement this kind of statistical data with richer and more nuanced qualitative data. For example statistics about school exclusions can be complemented and enhanced by qualitative data exploring critical issues that contribute to those school exclusions. Hence recent years have seen increasing numbers of child research studies adopting multiple perspective approaches. This does bring with it some challenges where different disciplines traditionally take different approaches and have to find ways of accommodating each other's perspective and valuing the knowledge each generates as being complementary not competitive. These complexities will be addressed in some of the research examples featured which engage with a range of different approaches and disciplines.

Research example: life as a disabled child

This research example is from a study which explored the perspectives of disabled children and factors that shape their lives. The author states that one of the overall aims was 'to consider "emancipatory" and "participatory" approaches from disability studies, feminism, anthropology and the new sociology of childhood' (Davis, 2009, 186) thus drawing on a number of disciplines, influences and techniques. The study used an ethnographic approach, combining participant observation with interviewing.

The full report can be found at

www.leeds.ac.uk/disability-studies/projects/children.htm (accessed 06/02/09).

Through participant observation, we aimed to contribute to and interpret everyday interactions in everyday places. This enabled us to work flexibly across a range of settings, including drama groups, symbols and signs classes, music therapy, physical education classes, outdoor activities, school trips, school playgrounds and out of hours leisure activities. We paid particular attention to developing good research relationships with the young people on their own terms. . . . After observing more than 300 children in their schools, we then involved 165 in more in-depth techniques. This included informal individual, paired or group interviews (depending on what the children wanted), as well as the compilation of written and visual accounts. These participants were diverse in terms of gender, ethnicity, social class, type of school and locality as well as impairment. Eighty-five of the young people invited the researchers to their home, after-school residential setting, summer play groups and after-school clubs/leisure activities.

1. Some disabled children have limited language skills and communication can be challenging for researchers. In Davis' study care was taken to cross-check with participants that researchers had not misinterpreted their answers or actions. This is illustrated by an incident that happened during a participant observation session.

Sharon, an [adult] assistant discusses a football match between Glasgow teams Rangers and Celtic with two disabled children, Bobby and John.
SHARON: Well, did you see the game last night?
JOHN: [a Celtic supporter] Aye, a wis there. Av almost lost ma voice shouting so much.

BOBBY: Aye.

SHARON: [looking at John as if to say, 'I don't believe him, watch this I'll catch him out'] Who won then?

BOBBY: [puts his hands in the air and gets frustrated] uh, uh, uh [like he's trying to spit something out but he just can't].

SHARON: See he doesn't know [said in a triumphal way to John, then whispers even though Bobby still can hear her] a don't think he really knows what's going on, a really don't think he understands.

Pause for thought

Before we go any further with this research example, stop for a moment to examine your own reactions. What are you thinking at this moment? Do you agree with Sharon that Bobby probably did not watch the football and is either pretending to have done so in order to be friends with John or genuinely doesn't understand what is being asked of him? Do you think there could be any other explanation? Read what happened next in the researcher's field notes . . .

[Bobby is really 'pissed off' with this and shakes his hands and head. John is sure Bobby watched the game because he spoke to him in signs earlier. Also, John thinks Bobby is finding it difficult to answer her question because the game was a draw and he can't say that word. He looks like he's going to give up, that he doesn't think he can make Sharon understand. John has had enough of Sharon so decides to intervene.]

JOHN: Na, na, I don't agree, Sharon. A think he knows.

BOBBY: Aye, aye.

SHARON: [still with disbelief] So what's the score?

JOHN: Look a know that he doesn't usually watch the football but a'm sure he seen this game. Ay Bobby now you tell me with signs, how many did Rangers score?

BOBBY: [puts up one finger]

JOHN: [without confirming that he's right] and how many did we [Celtic] get?

BOBBY: [puts up one finger]

JOHN: So the score was one–one?

BOBBY: Aye [said with triumph and gestures at Sharon with his hand as if to say 'so there'].

JOHN: And which team were lucky?

BOBBY: [Really laughing at the assistant because she's a Rangers supporter, he uses a word John has rarely heard him speak] Isss [us].

SHARON: [with a Damascus-type conversation tone in her voice] That's really good, Bobby, a nivir realized that.

⇨

Reflections on the research

Activity 1

Stopping to pause for thought in the middle of this extract highlighted the tensions that can arise where different people bring different approaches, different kinds of expertise and different perspectives to the same situation. Do you think the tensions were resolved satisfactorily? Can you anticipate any other issues that might arise?

Activity 2

The researcher stated that one of her aims was to consider 'emancipatory' and 'participatory' approaches from disability studies, feminism, anthropology and the new sociology of childhood. Could you find these different perspectives reflected in the extract? In this example, the researcher is collecting data via participant observation but also relying on the participation of others such as John, the disabled peer of Bobby, to interpret and mediate meaning. Would a different type of research, e.g. the kind of systematic observation favoured in early developmental psychology studies have generated the same data?

We have established that different disciplines do have different approaches and these shape the research methods they employ. Difference emanates from discrete theoretical frameworks underlying the various disciplines. For example ideology critique is central to the feminist approach and in particular the critique that research is based on a masculine way of looking at the world and therefore the ensuing knowledge that is generated is grounded in the male experience (Punch, 2005). Research techniques emerge from theoretical positions which reflect researchers' beliefs, values and dispositions towards the social world (Gray and Denicolo, 1998). Insider perspective is a driver not just for methods but a determinant of who undertakes certain types of research. Some argue (e.g. Shakespeare, 1996) that the inability of able-bodied researchers to orient their perspective to one of disability or white researchers to understand what it is to be black, compromises the validity of their research.

The same complexities apply to considerations of childhood. What does it mean to be a child? Should we think in terms of childhood or childhoods? What are the cultural implications? When is a child a child? When does a child cease to be a child? Childhood cannot be expressed in simple homogenous terms and an interdisciplinary approach accentuates difference and perspective. A young person has an identity as a young person but may also have multiple identities e.g. as black, female, gay or disabled.

Davis' research (the Tanzanian children's lives study) draws on interdisciplinary perspectives. In contrast, I now include a research example that depicts a single, discrete discipline – sociology – built on theories specific to that discipline. You can find examples of other discrete discipline research in the suggested further reading.

Research example: children's experiences of kinship

This research example is based on Jennifer Mason and Becky Tipper's study 'Being Related: how children define and create kinship'. You can find the full paper published in *Childhood*, 2008, 15, 4, 441–460. It is a study which explores sociological accounts of the negotiated, creative character of children's kinships through qualitative interviews with 49 children aged 7–12 in the north of England. Children were given disposable cameras prior to the interviews so that they could take photos of who mattered to them and that these photos could be used to stimulate discussion (a process known as photo-elicitation). Children were also encouraged to draw pictures and family maps to show how close or otherwise connections were.

Children expressed their ideas about who was 'proper' kin, who was 'like-family kin' and how all the different elements of kinship worked in their childhoods, e.g. how care, love and support influenced the quality and nomenclature of kinship. The authors argue (p. 444) that complexity of kinship is the norm and that conventional genealogical definitions based on heterosexual marriage, nuclear families or single cultural models are outdated.

> . . . many had close relatives who were separated or divorced. Some had half-siblings through a parent's previous relationship; most had half- and step-kin; many had relatives with cohabiting partners, or non-cohabiting partners, or ex-cohabiting partners, and in some cases these partners and ex-partners had children together; a few children had kin in same-sex relationships; some had kinship groups that included individuals from different religious and ethnic backgrounds; and some had kin they rarely saw because of geographical distance, or with whom they had lost contact due to family conflicts.
>
> One way for possible kin to earn 'proper' kinship status was *involvement in ritual, celebratory and routine aspects of family life*. Children spoke of whether or not potential kin attended family 'dos' and *how* they behaved at such events, particularly whether they were friendly and involved. . . . Being *friendly, nice, informal*, and perhaps most significantly *respecting children's orientations and interests*, was important to the children in our study when weighing up whether someone who was possible kin could be counted as 'proper' kin. This was especially significant when meeting new partners of 'proper' kin – such occasions being quite formative in children's judgement about whether or not they could be included as family. Children wanted to feel *physically* comfortable with potential kin, and indeed physicality – for example the freedom to touch or be cheeky with that person – was a significant part of many children's relationships.

However, kinship for children is not all about 'proper' relatives. Thirty-two (65 percent) of the children in our study specifically mentioned a special relationship that *seemed like family* with someone who was, genealogically speaking, unrelated to them. In all cases, this was clearly a conscious practice of drawing specific people close, by claiming them to be like family and this practice was always used by children to signify good or close relationships.

In our study, children's like-family kinship did not exclusively involve human relationships. In addition to their *own* household's pets, children frequently drew in 'proper' kin's pets (both living and dead) to their definitions of relatedness. When asked if there was anyone who he thought of as 'like family', Jake responded:

JAKE: Milly . . . because she is gran's rabbit and . . .

[INTERVIEWER]: She is kind of part of the family?

JAKE: Yes and so is Alf [gran's rabbit] and Bert [Jake's hamster] and my old rabbit Bonnie and my old guinea pig, what was it called . . . Bonnie and what?

SISTER: Clyde.

JAKE: Clyde. Well basically all my pets are like family. And all the family that has had pets have been really like family. [Jake, male, aged 9] (Mason and Tipper, 2008, 444–455).

Reflections on the research

Activity 1

Can you identify what gives this research study a distinct sociological perspective? Think about theories of kinship that are drawn on. Compare this study to the approach taken in the earlier example about Tanzanian children's lives.

Activity 2

On a large blank piece of paper write your own name in the centre. Radiating out from this, write down all your blood relatives. For each blood relative create a new spoke for all the kin they bring with them. Next go through each name and decide whether you regard them as 'proper' (P) kin or 'like-family' (LF) kin. Once you have finished this make a separate list of all the people who matter to you. How many of them are on your map? Where do the others fit in? How do you classify them? Are close friends 'like-family' or just friends? How different do you think your adult kinship map might be from a child's?

What are the challenges and tensions in multi-agency working?

We have spent time exploring academic disciplines but there is an important mass of research involving children that emanates from professional practitioners. Here, the most significant change in the last decade has been a move towards multi-discipline teams and multi-agency working with children. This reflects a political overhaul of children's services to bring about a 'joined up thinking' approach. High profile child abuse cases such as Victoria Climbie and Baby P have led to calls for better communication between different organizations working with children and a multi-agency approach to service provision.

To put this in context, let us take the example of a multi-agency approach to child development. Table 1 depicts some examples of professional workers, what their discrete role/expertise is and how this links to a multi-agency role.

This joined-up approach has facilitated opportunities for some interesting multi-agency research but also for evaluative research about the multi-agency working itself.

Table 1 Multi-agency working

professional	discrete role/expertise	multi-agency role
nursery nurse	social care and cognitive development	child protection, health and wellbeing
health visitor	general health and physical development	
child psychologist	child development and mental wellbeing	
physiotherapist	neuro-rehabilitation	

Research example: the MATCh project

The Multi-Agency Teamwork for Children's Services (MATCh) project (Anning et al., 2006) explored the different knowledge bases and practices which different professionals brought to their multi-agency teams, how these were shared and how new 'inter-professional knowledge' was created. This draws on Wenger's (1998) theory that new knowledge is created in communities of practice which complement processes of participation and reification (reification is a process where something abstract, such as knowledge, is represented in a tangible way e.g. through objects or documents). You can find the full research study in Anning, A., Cottrell, D., Frost, N., Green, J. and Robinson, M. (2006) *Developing Multiprofessional Teamwork for Integrated Children's Services*, Maidenhead: Open University Press. ⇨

The researchers collected their evaluation data via several methods:

- Documents (e.g. minutes of team meetings, agendas, team practice guide-lines, planning documents)
- Observation of team meetings
- One-to-one interviews with team members
- Critical incident diaries (critical incidents or dilemmas are good indicators of how teams work together but there was no guarantee any of these would happen when researchers were observing so participants were asked to keep diaries of critical incidents).

81 diaries were distributed to participants and 61 incidents were described from which the researchers identified the following themes (p. 20):

- Dilemmas of induction into a new team and threats to professional identity;
- Dilemma of changes of working practices – confidentiality/information sharing and workspace issues;
- Dilemmas of teams as community of practice – membership defined by jargon – exclusion of incomers;
- Dilemmas of liaison with professionals outside the team – inclusion;
- Differing values of professionals and differing values of professionals and service users; implications for decision-making; dilemmas of devolving/main-streaming of professional knowledge and skills.

From these incidents the researchers constructed some fictional practice scenarios for use in focus groups to further explore multi-team working issues and generate further data. Here is an example of one scenario (p. 21):

You are a psychologist working as part of a multi-agency team. One of the good things about your team is the way that everybody learns from everybody else so that you all broaden your skills. However, you are gradu-ally becoming aware that there is a downside to this, which is that your colleagues no longer seem to recognize that you have specific expertise that they do not have. There has been discussion of a particular case that you consider requires specialist input from a psychologist, but your colleagues disagree and do not seem to feel that your view should have more weight than anybody else's. What do you do?

Reflections on the research

Activity

This scenario was created from one of the themes identified in the critical incident diaries above (threats to professional identity). Study the remaining dilemmas and have a go at creating a multi-agency team scenario that could explore this in a focus group. What do you think about this kind of creative data generation technique? Would it work for you as a researcher? Would it work for you as a practitioner? Could it be adapted?

Pause for thought

It is interesting that this type of evaluative practice-based research does not involve children at any stage in the process and yet the purpose of effective professional inter-working is to improve outcomes for children. Is it always appropriate to involve children? There is a saying that has been coined by the disability movement 'nothing about us without us'. Ways of involving children would be to set up an advisory group to the project which included children or interview some children about their perceptions of different professional roles. An alternative perspective is that the adults might feel evaluating the efficacy of their inter-working raises issues that are too sensitive and their professional identities might be compromised if they involved children. What are your views?

Can I be your research partner?
The role of children as co-researchers in interdisciplinary child research

If we are looking for commonalities rather than difference in interdisciplinary child research then one of these is the inclination towards greater participation by children and to a growing use of children as co-researchers. In Chapter 6, I talk about children leading their own research. A consideration of the co-researcher role takes us part way on that journey.

Sometimes the terms 'children as participants' and 'children as co-researchers' are used interchangeably and this is not helpful. There is a distinct difference between children participating *in* an adult study and being co-researchers *of* an adult study. Participation can be anything from simply being data-generating participants, e.g. interviewees or questionnaire respondents to sharing in the active data collection. However, the co-researcher role is a partnership where the research process is *shared* between adults and children. A distinguishing element is that co-researchers can be involved in any number of the research phases from design to dissemination. If we were to think of a sandwich as a metaphor: participant researchers always form part of the filling, co-researchers also form part of the bread.

A typical 'bottom bread slice' contribution is being part of advisory and/or steering groups that help get a study off the ground and advise on the design of the study and on ethical and methodological issues for the duration of the study. 'Top bread slice' contributions might be helping to interpret the data, presenting findings at dissemination events or being involved in the writing up of the study. The 'filling' in-between constitutes the data collection and analysis phases. Here adults and children work as a team, commonly using their strengths and experience to best advantage. For example, if the joint study is about substance abuse, the team might conclude that it would be more effective for young people to interview other young people as this might generate richer data. Adults might be stronger in doing documentary/policy searches and interviewing practitioners. The young researchers might have an important role in helping to interpret the data for analysis. Best outcomes are achieved when adults and children work as a team.

Key differences between children as co-researchers in an adult study and children as researchers in their own right (supported by adults) are in size of contribution, ownership and responsibility. Adults ultimately own the study in the former scenario and must take responsibility for all aspects of it. They should also undertake the lion share of the work. If any of this is not happening then children are being exploited in their co-researcher roles. Adult researchers have a duty of care towards their child co-researchers and a moral imperative to acknowledge their contribution – in print.

The involvement of children as co-researchers is particularly suited to an interdisciplinary approach as several stakeholders are likely to have an interest in the outcomes.

Research example: Black young carers

In this research example, Adele Jones relates aspects of a study about the needs and experiences of Black children with caring responsibilities. Children and young people of different ages were involved as co-researchers in different activities. You can read the full research that Adele carried out with her colleagues in Jones, A., Jeyasingham, D. and Rajasooriya, S. (2002) *Invisible Families: The Strengths and Needs of Black Families in which Young People Have Caring Responsibilities*, Bristol: Policy Press and Joseph Rowntree Foundation. The extract below is taken from an article she wrote about the research study 2 years later (Jones, 2004):

> **Research Design** – An initial three-day consultation event familiarised children with the research process and enabled them to influence the areas of investigation necessary to reflect their experiences. The forum also dealt with the dynamics of young carers from different racial and cultural backgrounds searching out differences and commonalities.
>
> . . .

⇨

Ground rules set out the responsibility the adult researchers had for listening to and learning from children (as opposed to setting rules for children's behaviour). Exercises were devised to help children reflect both on their individual circumstances and to work collectively on the kinds of questions that would enable them to find out more about what being a carer means. The young people recognised that some of the information was sensitive and that they might feel vulnerable and exposed if they were sharing details about their home lives. They interviewed each other to identify the questions that it would feel 'safe' to answer. In these exercises and explorations young people were both informants and researchers. Some very rich information was produced and these early findings were fed back into the research process and used to develop the research design. Two interview schedules were devised, one for parents and other family members and one for children and young people. This process gave rise to questions about identity, religion and ethnicity, experience of family life, work children do to support disabled family members, the impact of tasks, the division and allocation of work, other factors affecting children and family life, experiences of services, wishes and aspirations.

Involving Young People in Collecting Data – Three young people were recruited as peer researchers. The peer researchers interviewed other young people while the adult researchers carried out interviews with parents, other family members and agencies. The role of peer researcher was considered appropriate for young people over the age of 16 because of the level of responsibility, maturity and skills needed for carrying out interviews. A four-day training course was developed in which the young people learned about research methods and developed interviewing skills. Interactive methods such as role play and video recording sessions were used.

. . .

Peer researchers were matched to research informants on the basis of gender, language and culture, young people's wishes and levels of confidence. Professional boundaries were established and the peer researchers equipped with skills and strategies for terminating interviews that they might find uncomfortable or distressing. (Jones, 2004, 199–210)

Reflections on the research

Activity 1

In this research extract, examples are given of young people as co-researchers being involved in design, planning and collecting data. How would you involve them in the process of analysing findings? Think about the context in which the interview data were collected and how these data might be interpreted differently by adults and children.

Activity 2

In what ways did this research highlight services the young people needed to access? How many different professionals did this have relevance to? Reflect on what this illustrates about the relevance of research studies to different disciplines.

Interview with Francis Omondi about the Tanzanian views of the children study

Reverend Francis Omondi is a leading figure in the Anglican Church of Kenya actively involved in Research on Poverty Alleviation (REPOA).

Mary: Is research involving children changing and if so in what ways?

Francis: It is hard to generalize this but with initiatives such as the Views of Children survey research with children is certainly changing. Initially children were taken as subjects to be studied and not participants. The level of children's participation in the processes of the survey was a learning experience that researchers planning to involve children in research need to take into account. First of all children were thrilled to be engaging with adult researchers instead of being given instructions. This made them feel relaxed. Secondly the aspect of engaging children in selection of research topics is one area that needs to be undertaken carefully. In some ways power plays between adults and children tend to take precedence favouring adults especially when adults have more information than children. This information could be about resources to be used in the study, research needs at the time or even who would be interested in the study results. Through the experience gathered from the Views of Children survey use of innovative ways of doing research with children works in Tanzania. A range of child friendly participatory tools can be used to engage children in research.

Mary: What do you think the rest of the world can learn from the kind of research involving children being carried out in Tanzania?

Francis: There are three key lessons that the world can learn from the research involving children in Tanzania with reference to the survey. First it is evident that children being social actors in themselves need to be given space to participate meaningfully in research. This is demonstrated by the way they provide informed responses to issues that affect them. In some ways their responses were the opposite of what adults felt. Therefore one could see the diversity that children can bring in discourses that affect them. Secondly contrary to earlier feeling that culture can be a hindrance to child participation in research children overcame this barrier. One would have expected children to fear strangers whom they do not know. Instead they felt more relaxed and eager to learn from the strangers. A word of caution can be sounded here though, in rural areas it might take longer to create rapport with children. Thirdly it can be learned that the survey prepared some ground work for future meaningful research work with children.

Mary: In the Views of the Children study, several organizations were involved – the Tanzanian government, the Research on Poverty Alleviation (REPOA) and the Research and Analysis Working Group. What are the advantages (and disadvantages, if you think there are any) of this kind of cooperation?

Francis: It is interesting to see the interplay of partnership that can be created between policy makers and researchers. The advantage of this kind of partnership is that issues affecting children raised through research can easily feed into government processes. Though it is hard to expect that the government will automatically incorporate such issues into its programmes and budgets but the expectations are always high on this since they are partners. The second advantage is that ownership of the product is shared by all partners. Thirdly with such a partnership it is possible to ensure that research is conducted in a timely manner so that results come when they are needed. For instance in this case the survey came at a time when the government through its poverty monitoring system had commissioned larger Views of the people survey. Results of the survey are expected to feed into the poverty monitoring system. The fourth advantage that can be experienced in this kind of partnership is the shaping of survey instruments and overall quality of research. With the diverse mix of expertise expected in this kind of partnership quality of work is bound to improve. However, despite the advantages certain shortcomings might also arise. The organization and management of such a partnership is normally a challenge. Power plays would normally be expected with those with the highest voice carrying the day. Therefore for such partnerships to function effectively both parties have to work towards a common goal.

Key points

- Research involving children is becoming increasingly interdisciplinary.
- There is a multi-agency approach to children's services, and this itself is the subject of much research.
- It is important to get a global perspective on childhoods and children's lived experiences. There is much we can learn from the diversity of research involving children worldwide.
- There is a distinct difference between children participating *in* an adult study and being co-researchers *of* an adult study.

What really matters in any consideration of interdisciplinary approaches and multi-agency working is that it leads to better outcomes for children. Childhood itself is multi-faceted so it is unlikely that a single discipline approach could achieve those best outcomes. The different theoretical frameworks that underpin an interdisciplinary approach and multi-agency practice enrich understanding of children's lives. One of the main themes running through this book is the importance of researching and valuing difference, a central tenet of contemporary childhoods, which challenges assumptions and empowers the marginalized. It makes sense that the complexities of difference can best be explored from multiple perspectives and shared expertise.

Summary

This chapter has explored:

- The growing interdisciplinary nature of research involving children.
- Considered the diversity of research worldwide and the importance of adopting a global focus to research involving children.
- Examined what different disciplines bring to child research and how these can be interwoven to enhance our understanding of children's worlds.
- Reflected on multi-agency working in children's services and what we can learn from practice-based evaluative research.
- The emerging role of children as co-researchers and how this role differs from children as participant researchers.
- Reviewed research examples that illustrate the nature of interdisciplinary approaches to research involving children.

Suggested further reading

Barker, R. (2008) *Making Sense of Every Child Matters: Multi-professional Practice Guidance*, Bristol: Policy Press.

This is an accessible book which sets out the main trends of the different professions in children's services including practice issues and case examples from health, education, social work, playwork, children's centres and early years.

Montgomery, H. (2009) *An Introduction to Childhood: Anthropological Perspectives on Children's Lives*, Oxford: Blackwell.

This book looks at childhood through an anthropological lens, it give you an appreciation of a single discipline perspective as discussed in the chapter.

Woodhead, M. and Faulkner, D. (2008) 'Subjects, objects or participants? Dilemmas of psychological research with children'. In Christensen, P. and James, A. (eds) *Research with Children: Perspectives and Practices* (2nd edn), Abingdon: Routledge, pp. 10–39.

The Research Process Reviewed from a Children's Rights Perspective

4

Introduction and key questions

In this chapter I look at child research from a rights perspective, featuring illustrative studies about the exercising of those human rights but also discussing what rights children have in the research process itself. This extends to commissioning and funding of research, the formulating of research questions, data-collection techniques and dissemination of findings (please note that ethical considerations were discussed in Chapter 2). At each stage of the process I explore the impacts for participating children and how their rights are affected.

- How are children's rights and research connected?
- Whose research is it anyway?
- Which came first the chicken or the egg?
- How is research involving children being funded?
- Should children be paid for participating in research?
- What children's rights issues should we consider in data-collection techniques?
- How are children's rights affected in conflict zones?
- Did you forget to come back and tell us what happened?

How are children's rights and research connected?

The multiple definitions of childhood render conceptions of children's rights very complex. Within academic circles, children's rights are often discussed separately from human rights. However this separation is itself a rights issue and there are calls (e.g. Lenzer 2002, 207–208) for 'a re-integration of the isolated segments of the children's rights agenda within the frameworks of human rights'. Others such as O'Byrne (2003, 374) concur, maintaining that in so far as children are human, they are subjects of human rights standards and that age is irrelevant.

Not withstanding the tendency towards separation, a substantial amount of research flows out of children's rights agendas. Facilitating children's rights has still a long way to go and progress has been slow. Consider for a moment that it is two decades since the United Nations Convention on the Rights of the Child (1989) and one decade since UNICEF (1998) released the following information about our children.

A quarter of the world's children live in poverty. Childhood and poverty go together. In poorer countries such as Angola, which the UN claims is the worst place in the world to be a child, children under 15 constitute 48 per cent of the population. Globally, an estimated 120 million children aged 5–14 work full time while a further 130 work part time. More than 130 million of the 625 million children of primary school age in developing countries have no access to basic education. 183 million of the world's children weigh less than they should for their age, 158 million children under 5 are malnourished, 800 million lack access to health services and, in the poorest countries, preventable diseases such as diarrhoea kill 2 million children every year. (cited in Franklin, 2002, 1)

That was written 10 years ago – yes, change has indeed been slow in coming. So how can we ensure that children will not be facing similar circumstances a decade from now? A crucial step is the embracing of children's rights as full human rights and a championing of those rights in the research we collectively undertake. For example, research that probes issues around the 'reasonable' physical chastisement by parents on children would connect with a human rights concern and at the same time illuminate some aspects of contemporary childhoods that are affected by these actions. Another example might be research exploring the quality of children's play and leisure in the light of their entitlement to this as a human right.

Whose research is it anyway?

Alongside other basic rights such as entitlement to health, primary education and leisure time as set out in the United Nations Convention on the Rights of the Child (1989) is children's right to quality research about their childhood and their lives. Children were little more than objects in early child research studies but it does not follow that later childhood research is necessarily exploitation-free or quality-assured. Indeed, there has been much criticism about research that purports to make claims about children's views – and even generalize from them – when close inspection reveals that the population samples on which findings have been based were woefully unrepresentative and/or adult-centric. Some research fails to generate accurate data about children's views because the methodological design is too adult and misses children's radar. One example might be where questions on a child survey are framed about things that are too adult and not in the child participants' experience so the children can only respond in the negative thus skewing the data. Another example is where adult parameters do not take account of the reality of children's worlds – e.g. a research project about children's experiences of bereavement which only focuses on human bereavement and fails to take account of the profound effect that pet bereavement may have.

Even the latest technologically driven, young person targeted methods carry a cautionary caveat – for example data generated via online anonymous questionnaires in internet chat rooms – since it is impossible to know with certainty that a young person responded to the questions, or that one young person has not returned the questionnaire multiple times. Researchers have to make equally fine judgements about the reliability of their sources from postal questionnaires too. There is much to be said for methods which involve face-to-face interaction with young people even though these are time consuming and expensive. Group interviews are becoming increasingly popular because they access larger cohorts of young people at one research visit although care has to be taken that group dynamics and dominant personalities do not distort the findings. This takes us back to an earlier point about children's fundamental right to quality research about their lives and the responsibility of researchers to ensure that methods and tools are fit for purpose and data generated are valid and reliable.

Research example: *What Do They Know?*

What Do They Know? (Davey, 2009) is a research report about young people investigating their human rights. It was supported by the Children's Rights Alliance England (CRAE) and funded by the Big Lottery. To read the full report go to http://www.getreadyforchange.org.uk/campaigns/reports [accessed 11/02/09]. If you want to know more about CRAE the website is www.crae.org.uk [accessed 11/02/09].

In Davey's study, 1,362 children and young people completed an online survey and 346 children and young people took part in focus group interviews. The population sample was diverse in terms of age and geographical location and included travellers, disabled young people, young people in care and those who are lesbian, gay, bisexual or transgendered (LGBT). The research looked at six aspects of children's lives: respect and freedom; family and friends; health and safety; education; play and leisure; and crime and neighbourhood. Children and young people had strong ideas about what is important to them. They wanted to be respected and listened to. It was important to be part of a family structure and to live as part of a community. They also thought it was important to know about and be able to exercise their rights. Findings showed that very few children and young people actually knew about or understood their human rights. Even fewer knew what to do if their rights were violated. Here is an extract from the report:

Family and friends

Children and young people who had experienced homelessness or were in danger of becoming homeless said there should be more information about what accommodation and financial support is available to those who may have to leave their family home. This was a particular concern for LGBT young people, for although they faced the same problems as other homeless people, being gay was seen to add to their difficulties because they had to cope with family and friends coming to terms with their sexuality and possibly deal with homophobic behaviour from hostel staff or other homeless people. Children and young people with mental health difficulties living in hostels wanted professional counselling to be made available to help them deal with their problems – particularly if they had to leave their family home under difficult circumstances. Some hostels did provide this information through leaflets and posters, but children and young people also wanted a professional counsellor to be available in hostels, or at least on call, should they need immediate help. Without proper access to a trained counsellor, one young person said she often took her frustrations out on others who did not have the skills to deal with her depression. In so doing, she left herself vulnerable to getting thrown out of the hostel because of behavioural problems.

Figure 1 Drawing by a boy aged 11

. . . Lack of facilities for teenagers

One of the most pressing issues to emerge from the focus group findings concerned the lack of play and leisure facilities available to teenagers. Two in every five children and young people (40%) said that facilities in their area had closed down with the main reason being lack of resources. They suggested that short-term project funding has adverse implications for the scope and quality of provision, leading to problems with staff retention and possible closure. Caught between being too old for playgrounds but too young to go to clubs or pubs, many teenagers complained that there was often nothing for them to do on week nights or at weekends.

Figure 2 Drawing by a girl aged 10

Reflections on the research

Activity 1

Revisit the research example extract and think about the connection to children's rights. What was the significance of using children's drawings as one of the methods?

Activity 2

To what extent do you think bad behaviour is linked to children being bored, having nothing to do and nowhere to go? Do you think that the right to leisure facilities is a child's human right? If there were better play and leisure facilities do you think there might be less undesirable behaviour? If so, who is most at fault – adults or children?

Pause for thought

Consider this quote from the Mental Health Foundation (1998, 4):

> We claim to be a child-centred society, but in reality there is little evidence that we are. In many ways we are a ruthlessly adult-centred society where children are defined almost exclusively in terms of their impact on adult lives. Our adult-centred society has tried to contain and limit the impact of children on adult life by either excluding them from much of it or blaming them for disturbing it.

How does this quote relate to the issues raised in the *What Do They Know?* research example?

Which came first – the chicken or the egg?

There are many other aspects of children's everyday lives that we can look at from a rights' perspective. The right to fair and just treatment is a fundamental human right but one where children often draw the short straw. Sometimes it can be difficult to unpick what actions trigger events and whether original causes are inherent in children's behaviour or in the adult-dictated environments in which they are obliged to exist. It is not uncommon for children to take the blame for what is an adult-initiated problem. This is best explored through a concrete example. The number of school exclusions in Britain is increasing rapidly – and also the ages of exclusions are getting younger. Children in the UK start formal education much earlier than many of our European counterparts. Arguably, many children are not ready, either emotionally or in terms of their social maturity. If they start school before they are ready, have to sit and listen to formal instruction for long periods of time when they would rather be out playing, they may get frustrated and disaffected. This can lead to the kind of behaviours that ultimately result in school exclusions. How far back can we trace the origins of exclusionary behaviour and do we know whether it began as a chicken or an egg?

Research example: Attention Deficit (Hyperactivity) Disorder (ADHD)

Prescription rates for Ritalin, used to treat ADHD, are rising at an alarming rate. The greatest increase was in the 1990s decade. In 1991 prescription rates were around 2,000 and by 1999 had soared to 158,000 with the numbers still increasing into the 00s. The administering of this drug is in the adult domain and children have no control over when and how it is used. Research highlights some disturbing findings.

Reflections on the research

Activity 1

Read the following statements and consider the extent to which you agree or disagree and then reflect on what this is saying about children's rights to bodily wellbeing.

> Since the indicators for ADHD cover behaviours that are ostensibly quite innocuous (such as fidgeting, being easily distracted, disliking schoolwork, talking excessively and interrupting) concerns have been expressed that the diagnostic criteria read more like a crime sheet of child and adolescent behaviours objected to by adults than any genuine disorder. (Coppock, 2002, 143)
>
> There is a strong suggestion that boys and children and young people from ethnic minorities may be over-represented in diagnoses of ADHD, reflecting the institutionalisation of differential gendered and cultural expectations of behaviour. (Coppock, 2002, 144)
>
> There is no physical test that can detect the supposed existence of ADHD. There are no specific physical symptoms associated with it. The ADHD diagnosis is made by comparing the children's behaviours with a description of the disorder as defined and accepted by experts and practitioners in the field. (Breggin, 1998, 121)

Research has shown (Drug Enforcement Administration, 1995) that drugs such as Ritalin produce a zombie-like effect by inhibiting feeling and spontaneity which also results in obedience and conformity. There are serious ethical concerns about using 'chemical coshes' in this way. In 1978 Ritalin was declared a Schedule II drug – the most addictive in medical usage (Coppock, 2002). Side effects from Ritalin can be extensive with physical symptoms ranging from nausea, headaches and dizziness to mental health problems such as depression and psychotic episodes that lead to violent or bizarre behaviours. Thus the drug may, in some cases, be causing the very behaviours it is being prescribed to alleviate.

Activity 2

Consider this quote from a parent which appeared in the *Observer* newspaper on 9th April 2000 and make a list of how many human rights of the 5-year-old child might have been violated before, during and after being prescribed Ritalin.

> He was like something out of *The Exorcist*, or Damien in *The Omen*. He stabbed his brother in the foot with scissors. I was frightened to go to sleep sometimes. He used to demand the pills and was definitely addicted. I find it incredible they're giving a class A drug to a five-year-old.

Pause for thought

If an adult consults a doctor about being depressed, a doctor would talk through all the possible options for treatment, including alternatives to drugs such as counselling. A doctor would also advise an adult patient on possible side effects of any drugs and, unless action was taken under the mental health act to detain the patient against his or her will, then the final decision on whether to take anti-depression drugs would be the patient's not the doctor's. How does this compare with the rights of children?

Key points

- It is two decades since the United Nations Convention on the Rights of the Child and up to a quarter of the world's children still live in poverty.
- Children are human beings – children's rights are human rights.
- Research based on children's human rights is raising awareness about their powerless status and the ease with which adults can control and abuse them e.g. in legitimating physical assault and enforced imbibing of Class A drugs.
- Research helps give impetus to children's voice and to influence policy about the recognition of their rights.

How is research involving children being funded?

Organizations such as government departments, local authorities, research funding councils and children's charities are in a position to commission research with, about or by children. Generally, these organizations want to find out how they can improve children's lives, what services work best and least, how childhood is changing and how practices can best be adapted to benefit children. As such, they are acting on behalf of stakeholders and have a responsibility to uphold children's rights. Optimally, organizations will include stakeholders from the outset. It is a rights issue that organizations adequately represent their stakeholders. This might involve surveying them for views, opinions and ideas for relevant research to commission or inviting them to focus group discussions. Sometimes stakeholders are involved in reviewing research proposals and invariably they are involved in advisory groups for commissioned projects. I would argue strongly that all these stages should include children. While this is beginning to happen in some organizations, children are still largely excluded from research commissioning processes. The recently published and much broadcast research inquiry 'A Good Childhood' (Layard and Dunn, 2009) was commissioned by the Children's Society to undertake an extensive examination of the state of contemporary childhood. The inquiry review panel consisted of ten members: seven professors (one of whom was also the Children's Commissioner for England), two clerics and a programme manager representing the Children's Society. While the study collected data from innumerable children, children were not involved in the commissioning or design stage, nor was there any advisory group or steering committee specifically convened to work with the Review panel that might have included children.

The kind of child research undertaken is also very dependent on funding. Research that explores children's rights can be controlled, to a large extent, by those holding the funding reins. It is interesting that the majority of children's rights research is funded by NGOs and children's charities – e.g. the Good Childhood Inquiry was funded by the Children's Society, UNICEF funded the 2007 inquiry into children's wellbeing. The UK government funds a considerable amount of research around what children should be learning in school and their behaviour in public spaces but very little about their right to a balanced education or their right to play and leisure. At the same time the government makes token gestures such as the appointment of a Children's Commissioner to champion children – an appointment with a tiny budget and no political teeth. There are considerable societal power structures and inequalities to be engaged with before children's rights can become pivotal to children's research agendas.

Activity 1

The inquiry panel of the Good Childhood study explored seven self-determined 'key themes' of childhood: family, friends, lifestyle, values, schooling, mental health and inequality. Do you think these would have been the key themes that children might have decided were the most important to explore? If you have children of your own or are in close contact with any, ask them what they think the most important aspects of childhood are and see if they come up with anything different. *A Good Childhood* (Layard and Dunn, 2009) is the most comprehensive and, at the time of writing, most recent study of childhood in the UK. It was undertaken almost a decade into the twenty-first century with a mantra of children's rights yet children still became the objects of its inquiry not the drivers. There are many good things that have come out of this inquiry, not least strong words about child poverty and inequality but I am saddened that something which is being hailed as a landmark report in some quarters appears to have missed an important boat. For example, one part of the report looks at how children spend their time over a year (average hours per week including school holidays). Instead of getting together with children to involve them in how they would design categories to measure this in ways that reflected childhood today in the here and now, the panel chose to use existing research by ONS Time User Survey undertaken in 2001. *A Good Childhood* was written in 2009, so findings about children's use of time were based on research that was 8 years old – half of a childhood! We know from other research (e.g. Buckingham and Bragg, 2009) that the way children occupy their time has changed significantly in the past 5 years, something that seems to have escaped the 'adult' panel of the Inquiry. The more substantive point is that children were not involved in the whys and hows of researching children's time use. There is nothing in the data produced by the Inquiry which relates to how children would *choose* to spend their time, or what they consider their *rights* to be in relation to their time.

Very little research is ever cost neutral. Somebody has to pick up the bill and unless you happen upon a philanthropic benefactor or a group of enthusiastic volunteers then some form of funding is going to be needed. Research involving children is sometimes underwritten by children's charities and organizations as well as government departments and research councils. However, funding rarely comes without strings attached. Some strings are more obvious than others and we have to act responsibly to ensure that children are not exploited. For example, there has been an increase in the number of market research companies funding research involving children for commercial purposes. While this in itself is not necessarily injurious, the manipulation and 'cherry picking' of findings to support marketing perspectives can be.

Activity: a funding scenario

A company that makes bottled water decides to fund some research about the benefits of children drinking water. They plan to do this by commissioning a children's organization to manage the research. On the surface this may appear philanthropic but the company also has a vested interest in the outcome of the research because findings may increase sales of their bottled water. They organize high-profile press releases to coincide with the publication of findings and turn up at the launch with product logo T-shirts and caps for children to wear along with billboard advertising of a funky new-shaped bottle for their water specially designed to fit into children's school lunch boxes. In future advertising campaigns they adopt a strap line that exploits the research findings 'Research X shows Y. Give your kids a head start with [name of bottled water product]'. Consider what the implications are in this funding scenario.

Should children be paid for participating in research?

Whether children are involved in adult studies or their own, the complex issue of payment looms large. There are several schools of thought. The first asserts that children are very busy people and their time is precious. Participating in research means they are usually giving up something else and should be compensated for their time. This is rarely in the form of actual cash but store tokens are common, or an organized outing as a treat. Some children find these kinds of payments condescending and would prefer to have a 'research wage'. An alternative perspective is that children benefit from participating in research – e.g. through their self-development and the enhancement of their voice – and that these intrinsic rewards are sufficient. Another perspective is that children would participate just to get payment, would not be committed to the aims of the research and would therefore produce unreliable data. Some of these positions align with the payment situation for adults. Not all adults get paid for involvement in research, some volunteer. However, professional researchers are always paid, either because it is their job and they are drawing a salary or they are being funded. Most funded research will offer some kind of payment to adults who volunteer participation beyond filling in a simple questionnaire. If adults participate in research that involves substantial investment of their time (e.g. travelling to venues for interviews) or risk to their wellbeing (e.g. drug trials) they nearly always receive payment. Where children are concerned it is imperative that their participation in research does not leave them out of pocket, so as an absolute minimum, all travel costs and resource costs should be met. Moreover, every effort should be made to cover the cost of travel in advance, it is not always easy for children to pay up front and claim back the cost later. All these points link back to children's rights, here we are concerned with their right to have their time valued and their right to choose how they spend their free time.

Activity

As yet, there is no universal ruling on the payment of child research participants, it is something that is determined by the principal researcher, and if possible by an advisory or steering group. Ethics committees will sometimes want to know what the payment arrangements are, if any.

Put the following statements in order according to which are nearest to your own personal perspective on payment for children and which are furthest from it.

'I don't think children should be paid for research, they would just come for the money, mess around and then go and spend it on fags.'

'Children should not be paid for research if it is during school time as they would otherwise be doing lessons but if it is at weekends or evenings then they should.'

'I don't think you should give children cash as they might spend it on alcohol or cigarettes or something inappropriate, but it's good to give them book tokens or vouchers.'

'Time is money. It's no different for children than it is for adults.'

'Children get kudos from being involved in research, they don't need payment.'

'If you give children cash their parents might appropriate it, so my advice is to give them a toy or a book or something that would only be of value to a child.'

Once you have ordered the quotes, reflect on why you have ordered them in this way. Does it tell you anything about your views on contemporary childhood and children's rights issues?

What children's rights issues should we consider in data-collection techniques?

If we are going to research children and childhood in any meaningful way, we have to consider carefully what methodologies we employ. In adult research, when qualitative practice-oriented approaches, such as action research, first made an appearance there was sceptism from positivist, scientific groups that such methods could ever produce rigorous research. Adjectives like 'soft' research found their way into critical vocabulary. We have to be careful that research involving children does not suffer a similar fate. We cannot do child research without obtaining data from children. Even when data are collected by adults, this still requires engagement with children. Denigration (e.g. Alderson and Morrow, 2004) that some child research is not fit for purpose has arisen because methods do not generate accurate data. This is because the methods employed are either outside children's experience or are overlain with power dynamics that get in the way. At the heart of this is imperfect communication. Adults and children exist in parallel spheres where the simplest of enquiries can go awry – as in the example here of an interview where an adult researcher is investigating family relationships with a child (Greene and Hill, 2005, 10),

> Q: How close are you to your grandfather?
> A: Well, not very close really: I live in Dublin and he lives in Offaly.

Not all examples are as humorous as this and can lead to seriously flawed, mediated findings being disseminated. This in itself is an infringement of children's rights.

There is no reason why tried and tested data-collection techniques such as observation, interview and surveys should not work well in child research provided the methods used are child-centred and age and context appropriate. James (1999, 244) maintains that 'observation, participation and interviewing all entail implicit assumptions about children's competency . . . tools of the trade they might be, but they are far from value free'. With regard to interview situations, Westcott and Littleton (2005, 141) remind us 'It is easy to forget that children may rarely be spoken to, or seriously listened to, unless they have done something "wrong"'. Data-collection methods need to be about creating joint meaning making so that distinctions can be made between children's lives as lived, experienced and told (Westcott and Littleton, 2005, 153). If we are researching children's lived experiences then they have a right to determine that our methods will engender accurate accounts.

Research example: naturalistic observation

The Cultural Ecology of Young Children (CEYC) was a project which aimed to generate data about young children's typical everyday lives. The reference for the full report is Tudge, J. R. H., Hogan, D. and Etz, K. (1999) 'Using naturalistic observations as a window into children's everyday lives: an ecological approach'. In Berardo, F. M. (series ed.) and Shehan, C. (vol. ed.) *Contemporary Perspectives on Family Research, Vol 1. Through the Eyes of the Child: Re-visioning Children as Active Agents of Family Life*, Stamford, CT: JAI Press, pp. 109–132.

The extract that follows is taken from a later paper written by Tudge and Hogan (2005, 108–109) as it provides a useful summary.

> In the CEYC project, we are interested in the typical everyday experiences of children, putting no restrictions on where the child goes or on the people who interact with the child. We follow each of the children in our study (who are all between 28 and 48 months of age when the study begins) for twenty hours over the course of a week. We do this in such a way that we cover the equivalent of a complete day in their lives, observing on one day when the child wakes up, another day the hours before he or she goes to bed, and on other days during the hours in between. Using this technique, we get a good sense of the types of activities in which the child is typically involved, the partners in those activities, the roles taken, and so on.
>
> . . .
>
> Although each observer observes for twenty hours, data are only gathered during a thirty-second period every six minutes. The remainder of the time is spent coding and writing field notes, while continually tracking what the participants are doing.
>
> . . .
>
> The last two hours of observation are videotaped. . . . Although videotapes clearly have their uses, we do not film the entire twenty hours and base our codes on the taped activities. There are a number of reasons for this. One is that the presence of a camera is likely to change people's behaviours more than does the simple presence of an observer. Equally important, however, is the fact that the camera's field of vision is so much more limited than the human eye. Our interest is mostly on the child, but we also need to know what activities are going on that the child is not currently involved in. These are the activities that are available to the child, and it is important to know what these activities are, regardless of the child's participation. Moreover, because we are interested in knowing who initiated the activities in which the child participates, and how the child became involved, we cannot ignore activities in which the child is not yet engaged.

Reflections on the research

Activity

The research described above is 10 years old. Are the principles still current? For example do you think that collecting data for 30 seconds every six minutes is likely to be an accurate representation of typical behaviour? If data is gathered for 20 hours over one week but only 30 seconds recorded each 6 minutes this equates to a little over 3 hours of codeable data. How different might it have been if the whole of the 20 hours had been coded and analysed? Is there a rights issue here? Would you adapt any of this methodology if you were undertaking naturalistic observation of young children today? Consider how long you might collect data for, whether you would use a video camera and what the ethical issues might be.

Research example: interview techniques

Interviews are commonly used to collect data from children and young people. There are different types of interviews and, as stated earlier, matching method to participant age and context is essential. The first type to consider is structured interviews commonly used when researchers are interested in standardized answers. They share some of the characteristics of a survey but are administered verbally so are not restricted by particpants' age or literacy competence. The following extract (Kellett, 2005, 64–65) illustrates the process.

> Let us suppose you are interested in children's views about school lunches. . . . Ideally, you frame the question in a way that allows some qualification of response but without this being too free otherwise you end up with lots of different answers that are difficult to standardise. Limiting the choices available is one form of structure.

> Staying with our example of school lunches, let us look at some possible phrasings of a first question about the size of portions.

> *Do you think the portions are big enough?*
> *Do you think the portions are too small?*
> *Do you think the portion size is generous?*
> *Are you still hungry when you've finished your lunch?*

Even thought these all invite a yes or no response they are subtly different. By asking 'do you think the portions are *big* enough' the interviewer is subtly suggesting that the portions are big but are they big *enough*? By asking if they are *too small* the interviewer is planting in the interviewee's mind the idea that portions are small and asking if they think they are *too* small. Introducing the word *generous* has a similar affect and asking if the child is *still hungry* is planting an expectation in the respondent's mind that school lunches leave you hungry. This is what we call question framing bias and often it operates at a subconscious level when researchers hardly even realise they are being biased in the way they present a question. A much more neutral question would be,

What do you think about the size of the portions you get?

However, this is more open-ended and is likely to invite lots of different answers. It is difficult to standardise such wide-ranging answers. . . . The way forward lies in giving interviewees a wider range of choice than yes/no but *limiting* this choice.

Would you say that the portion size is about right, too small or too large?

Reflections on the research

Activity
Think of a topic that you might like to interview children about e.g. their views on learning a foreign language at primary school. Design 2 or 3 questions that will elicit responses you can standardize making sure they are not biased questions. Consider what children's rights might be affected by flawed research methods.

By contrast, unstructured interviews are open-ended and designed to elicit individual and richly descriptive responses. They are used when researchers want to understand opinions and/or behaviour at a more complex level without pre-imposing any categories of response. There are no set questions or pre-determined framework for the responses. The role of the researcher is to gently probe when it is appropriate and to invite the interviewee to elaborate, qualify or clarify when necessary. A good example of this type of interviewing technique follows in Chapter 5 with Sam Punch's research about children in rural Bolivia.

Semi-structured interviews are the most common and very popular in research with children. Here, researchers have a small core of pre-determined questions or topic areas that they want to ask at some point during the interview, but beyond that it is unstructured and unscripted. These core questions would not be asked in any specific order and may not even need to be asked directly if the answers crop up in the general conversation. The most important characteristic of a semi-structured interview is flexibility. This gives the interviewer the freedom to pick up on individual responses and take the questioning in different directions where appropriate. This can often take the interview off in interesting and unexpected directions.

Research example: semi-structured interviews

The following extract was an opening question in a semi-structured interview in some research about school lunches (Kellett, 2005, 68)

I: *What are the school lunches like here?*

R: *They're awful. I wanted to stop having them and bring a packed lunch but my mum won't let me.*

Already, the researcher has an interesting trail that she or he may choose to pursue or let go. Choice was one of the pre-established themes for this interview but this was in relation to the food choice and here, already is an interesting situation about who exercises power and control over the choice of school or packed lunches. The researcher could turn away from this trail by following up with, *Why do you say they're awful?* Or, she or he could pick up on the response and probe more deeply with questions such as, *Why do you think your mum won't let you have packed lunches?* (this in turn, could lead on to other response trails such as having to have free school meals or mums thinking children get a 'good, hot dinner' when in fact they're frequently stone cold etc.)

Reflections on the research

Activity

If you had been the researcher in what direction would you have steered the interview? You might like to think about what the purpose of the interview is and what kind of data you are trying to generate. Are there any rights issues here?

In group interviews (or focus groups) researchers gather data from several children at the same time. The role of the researcher is different in a group interview and the process is less like an interview and more like a 'guided discussion'. The researcher is a facilitator who is interested in group interaction as well as the statements being made. Researchers guide the topics of discussion and, depending on the degree of structure required, the questions. An advantage of asking questions in group situations is this can sometimes access information that would not be as forthcoming in individual interviews or that only materializes because of transactional dialogue.

The growing emphasis on children's rights has resulted in much more participatory research by children which calls for creative methods. A crucial distinction is that participatory research assists the process of knowledge production rather than data gathering.

> [participatory methods are] an integral part of a reconceptualization of 'childhood' which recognizes that children have their own 'child cultures'. . . . This has led to a critical examination of traditional research methods and a search for methods that can serve as tools or frames for children's experiences to be articulated in the research process. (Veale 2005, 253)

Some examples of creative methods are artwork; drama; story games; photography; ranking activities; songs; mapping games. There are many others and children themselves are brilliant at inventing new ones.

Research example: storytelling

Here is an example of a story game method from Veale's (2005, 260) participatory project in a community in Rwanda. It depicts one of the stories about genocide. In these story games each line is contributed by a different child.

> We ran away and lost our parents. – I was hungry. – I was separated from my parents. – We found a child. – Others died. – There were a lot of bullets shot. – We moved by running. – They brought us into an orphanage. – We met nice people. – When we reached home a child died, – was found, – was buried. – We experienced terrible things. – We met those who carried us. – They brought us back home. (Reunified children's group aged 13–17 years)

Reflections on the research

Activity

Children's drawings are increasingly being used as a creative method to research children's experiences and generate particularly rich data when children are invited to talk about their drawings. Consider how the above data might have been collected through children's drawings instead of, or additional to, the story telling method above. If you want to see some examples of children's drawings as research data there are plenty in the Davey's (2009) study *What Do They Know?* alluded to earlier in the chapter.

Key points

- Children have a fundamental human right to quality research about their child-hood and their lives (UNCRC, 1989).
- Children are rarely involved in the commissioning of research or how research funding should be allocated.
- Children's time is precious. Consideration has to be given to payment for children's involvement in research particularly if they are part of adult studies.
- Methods used in research involving children have to be child-appropriate and mindful of children's rights.
- Some examples of creative methods for involving children in research include: artwork; drama; story games; photography; ranking activities; songs; mapping games.

How are children's rights affected in conflict zones?

Children's rights are violated when they are caught up in war zones and conflict situations. Fundamental rights such as accessing an education, the right to play safely and be free from violent assault are routinely overridden.

Research example: *Knowing Children*

A resurgence of violence in South Thailand in 2004 had a major impact on children's daily lives. In conjunction with UNICEF Thailand, the Thai NGO Knowing Children and its three partner organizations, Friends of Thai Muslim Women, Luk Riang Group and the Young Muslim Association of Thailand, conducted a research study into children's experiences called *Knowing Children*. It was published in 2008. You can download the full report from www.knowingchildren.org or from the UNICEF Thailand website www.unicef.org/infobycountry/Thailand [accessed 17/02/09].

This was a large research study: 2,357 children living in the conflict-torn southern-most provinces participated and 283 children living in conflict-free central Thailand formed a control group for the research. Nine child-friendly research methods were used to elicit a rich source of qualitative and quantitative data.

- Children's drawings of 'good' and 'bad' people and good/bad experiences.
- Visual stimulus pictures with associated questions.
- Neighbourhood maps of safe and unsafe places.

- Attitude survey with statements that children responded to.
- Listing of responses to a particular phrase.
- Sentence completion from a starter phrase.
- Interviews.
- Drawings and/or essays on 'my school' and 'my vision of peace'.
- Flower of peace (a protection tool that allowed children to finish on a positive note).

One part of the report concerned the impact on children's school experiences and children's voices are clearly evident in the findings quoted in the following extract (UNICEF Thailand, 2008, 11).

> In the essays, references to the unrest and its effects on schools were vivid and disturbing, as were the comments children wrote when explaining their drawings of good and bad experiences. For example, a 7-year-old Buddhist boy from a village in Yala that was neither a Red Zone nor associated with a high rate of violence, wrote:
>
> *'I want soldiers and police officers to come take care of my school so that we can study without worrying about when the insurgents will show up and hurt us. When there are soldiers around, there's more peace and security. Then both teachers and students won't have to fear so much.'*
>
> Similarly, a 15-year-old girl from the same province wrote:
>
> *'My school used to have many beautiful things and also kind teachers. It is also a big school and I am glad to study here. But my school was burned down and I helped put out the fire.'*
>
> And a 10-year-old Buddhist boy, also from Yala, gave a detailed description of the way his education was being disrupted:
>
> *'My school is full of terror. The insurgents come to agitate and threaten us often. My parents say that they want to create a situation so that everyone's scared. They want us to be so scared that we stop going to school. They cut down all the trees in my school so there is no more shade. I'm jumpy on my way to school because I don't know when they might come and really hurt us. The teachers ask to close the school often because the insurgents create the situation. Both teachers and parents are worried about the safety of teachers and pupils. This happens very often.'*
>
> In talking about his drawing of bad experiences, a 9-year-old boy told the field workers that on school days he would sometimes arrive to find the school closed. Many other children mentioned school closures. Others told of their schools being burned down and teachers shot. As a 14-year-old boy bluntly explained: 'Before, my school was a comfortable place. But now the evil insurgents have completely burned it down so I have to study in a tent.'

Reflections on the research

Activity 1

Take a little time to reflect on the plight of children caught up in conflict zones. Try and think of all their rights which might be negated in a single day, from getting up in the morning to going to bed at night. Does this influence your views on the importance of research incorporating children's rights perspectives?

Activity 2

At the end of the *Knowing Children* report eight recommendations were made:

1. Promote awareness of children's rights and child protection in Pattani-Malay and Thai languages among civil society and all armed groups and forces, including the military, police and Village Security Teams.
2. Focus peace-building education and activities on children in both state schools and religious schools, as well as out-of-school children, through formal and non-formal education programmes.
3. Promote implementation of the Ministry of Education's regulation banning corporal punishment in schools, and support development of alternative disciplinary techniques.
4. Strengthen mechanisms for reporting and responding to violence against children within families, communities and schools.
5. Ensure that child protection services and organizations have appropriate resources to identify and respond to cases, taking into account the unique nature of the situation in the southern border areas.
6. Design programmes to address the emotional stress that children experience living in the provinces affected by the unrest, and ensure these programmes also build upon the children's natural resiliency.
7. Promote drug prevention and rehabilitation programmes on the principles of harm reduction, and strengthen diversion and rehabilitation programmes for children as alternatives to legal proceedings.
8. Ensure that schools and communities are designated as 'zones of peace' by reducing the presence of arms among all parties.

How do you think these recommendations should be implemented in the best interests of children and in pursuit of their rights? Think about how children might be involved in the implementation process.

Pause for thought

Imagining a peaceful future

> I want to have pencils, erasers, pencil sharpeners, colours and kind teachers.
> I want to live in [my] district because it is a city of haze and beautiful
> flowers. I want every province to be like [mine] because there's no violence.
> I don't want any bad thing to happen in my district. I pray that there's peace.
> I want Thais to love one another and be united. (9-year-old girl from Yala,
> Thailand, *Knowing Children*, p. 30)

Is any of this unreasonable for a 9-year-old child to crave? Do you regard these aspirations
as fundamental children's rights?

Did you forget to come back and tell us what happened?

The dissemination of child research brings us full circle back to an original
premise made at the beginning of this chapter: children have a fundamental
human right to quality research about their childhood and their lives. Therefore they have a fundamental right to appropriate dissemination of that
research. When researchers collect data with or from children they raise
expectations in those children that some benefit may accrue to them either
through greater understanding and tolerance of their views or changes that
will improve their lives. Once a study is finished, perhaps a report has been
written, some researchers are already moving on to the next project. Not
enough time is given to dissemination and not enough funding is allocated to
this important process. So whom should we be targeting and how?

The first target group, and the one most often overlooked, is children themselves, especially children who have participated in the research. If you talk to
children they are very forthcoming about the endless consultations (including
de rigueur balloons!) they engage in that appear to lead to nothing. The tales
of woe abound of researchers who spend a couple of weeks at their school,
come to interview them in their homes or video-record them at their youth
centre and then the children never find out what happened next. Better ethical
practice has started to reduce the incidence of this but it is still a concern.
There is an ethical duty (and moral imperative) to feedback findings to
children who have participated in adult research. This dissemination has to be

at an accessible level. Good researchers will produce different types of feedback. With children this might be going back and talking to them about the outcomes, preparing a summary in child-friendly language to send to them, or even better inviting them to be part of the dissemination by joining panel discussions and seminars.

Adult groups to target for research about children's rights are those groups who can bring about change – politicians, child workforce professionals, academics and the media. Tailored dissemination is the most effective so, while a lengthy formal report might be appropriate for government departments, it is unlikely to woo a newspaper. DVDs and custom-designed websites are becoming increasingly popular and effective forms of research dissemination.

Interview with Dr Ciara Davey about children's rights

Dr Ciara Davey is Senior Children's Rights Investigator, Children's Rights Alliance for England (CRAE), UK.

Mary: Can you tell me a little about the work of CRAE?

Ciara: The Children's Rights Alliance for England (CRAE) protects the human rights of children by lobbying government and others who hold power, by bringing or supporting test cases and by using regional and international human rights mechanisms. We provide free legal information and advice, raise awareness of children's human rights, and undertake research about children's access to their rights. We mobilise others, including children and young people, to take action to promote and protect children's human rights. Each year we publish a review of the state of children's rights in England. The Children's Rights Alliance for England (CRAE) has monitored the implementation of the UNCRC in England since its ratification by the UK Government in 1991. Involving children and young people (aged 17 and under) has always been central to CRAE's work, but the Get ready for Geneva project has allowed us to develop this much further. In June 2007, young Get ready for Geneva volunteers (aged between 7 and 17 years of age) began a nationwide children's rights investigation, discovering from their peers how well children and young people's human rights are respected, protected and realised in England. In June 2008, a delegation of

12 children and young people presented the findings of this investigation to the UN Committee on the Rights of the Child at its pre-session working group in Geneva. *What Do They Know? Investigating the human rights concerns of children and young people living in England* takes a more in-depth look at the evidence both given and collected by children and young people through the Get ready for Geneva children's rights investigation.

Mary: What part do you think research can play in the advancement of children's rights?

Ciara: One of the aims of the Get ready for Geneva project was to engage children and young people in the international reporting process for the United Nations Convention on the Rights of the Child (UNCRC), and support them to carry out their own human rights advocacy and campaigning. One of the principles of the project was to empower children to conduct research on their rights as a means of educating and ensuing that the research was grounded in the real life experiences and perspectives of children and young people. We were also keen to capitalize on the energy and passion exhibited by young people who are often keen to speak out and take action on issues that affect them. Our young campaigners, through training, action and experience, have gained skills in project management, evaluation, communication, site development, social research methods, research analysis, report writing, legal advocacy, campaigning, promotion, public speaking, training delivery, recruitment, negotiation and deliberation. Peer-led research has also enabled our young volunteers to get a glimpse of the multiple and varied experiences of what it is really like for a child to grow up in England today.

CRAE is now supporting our young campaigners to use their findings from the *What Do They Know?* report to inform three national human rights campaigns, focusing on representations of young people who are named and shamed in the media, counselling and confidentiality, and the right to education for young refugees and asylum seekers. You can keep up to date with the campaigns by visiting CRAE's Get ready for change! website at http://www.getreadyforchange.org.uk.

Mary: In your opinion what are the three most important children's rights issues that need more research?

Ciara: It is extremely difficult to prioritise the three most important children's rights issues for children in England today not least because the philosophy behind the UNCRC is that all children's rights are equally important, interlinked and interdependent. That said three issues which are amongst the most egregious breaches of children's rights and which were highlighted in the concluding observations from the UN Committee on the Rights of the Child include:

1. Issues relating to the use of physical restraint against children housed in young offender institutions and secure training centres and the use of force in schools.
2. The lack of awareness, training and availability of information on children's rights and the need to incorporate the UN Convention on the Rights of the Child into domestic law.
3. The negative stereotypes of children and young people in the media and in particular, the use of naming and shaming techniques to demonise children.

For the same reason as outlined above, it is very difficult to identify what are the three most important children's rights issues from the 'What do they know?' report as the data is so wide-ranging. If I absolutely had to choose the three most pressing issues which might require further research they would be the following:

1. More research is needed on the provision of child-friendly complaint mechanisms in services used by children such as schools, dentists, doctor surgeries and the courts. Our investigation showed that despite very vocal concerns about discriminatory treatment, few children and young people raised concerns or complaints. Those that were aware of complaints mechanisms often felt unable to use them – because they felt they would not be believed, because they felt there was no likelihood of their complaint being upheld because procedures were not independent, or because 'complaining' was not encouraged.
2. More research is needed on what training professionals who work with children (like doctors, healthcare workers, school teachers) receive in the area of children's rights. A recent report by CRAE entitled *Beyond Article 12* found that knowledge about the UNCRC in local authorities, from strategic level to grass roots delivery, is far from consistent, and that children's rights do not routinely inform strategic planning or day-to-day work. The Committee on the Rights of the Child has also raised concerns about training for professionals on children's rights and having more of a say was the number one issue children and young people wanted to change about their school. Further research on this issue could produce recommendations to address the current deficit in children's rights training opportunities.

3. More research is needed on access to advocates for refugee and asylum seeking children. Our research suggested that this particular group of children often encounter major difficulties accessing a range of rights such as being able to use advice services, social services and appropriate healthcare, and they were concerned about the impact of living conditions on their short and long-term health. Young refugees and asylum seekers also reported feeling victimised, citing not only the media but also age disputes with the Home Office or local services, lack of identification papers and fewer educational opportunities than other children and young people as the main reasons for this. Research examining access to advocates could possibly address some of these difficulties by making firm recommendations on where legislation and policy needs to be strengthened to ensure these children have access to advocates who can represent their best interests.

Key points

- Violations of children's rights are graphically evident where they are caught up in war zones and conflict areas.
- Children have a fundamental right to appropriate dissemination of research about them – too often researchers overlook reporting back to participating children themselves.

The importance of constructing research involving children from a rights perspective cannot be underestimated. It foregrounds children's rights as human rights and challenges the legitimacy of research enquiry which does not take these into account. It emphasizes the centrality and agency of children throughout the research process irrespective of whether the research is about, with or by children. It presents an opportunity to improve the life chances of all children.

Summary

This chapter has:
- Outlined a philosophical rational for research involving children from a children's rights perspective.
- Reviewed the processes of research involving children such as commissioning, funding and methodologies from a children's rights perspective.

- Explored some data-collection techniques in child research and discussed how these can be orientated to a rights perspective.
- Illustrated some research examples that illustrate creative approaches to research involving children.
- Reflected on conflict situations where children's rights are violated and discussed how research can make a difference.
- Considered optimal ways to disseminate research about children.

Suggested further reading

Jans, M. (2004) 'Children as citizens: towards a contemporary notion of child participation', *Childhood*, 11, 1, 27–44.

This article discusses children as active citizens and engages with the tensions of children being represented as autonomous individuals on the one hand and objects of protection on the other.

Lundy, L. (2007) '"Voice" is not enough: conceptualising Article 12 of the United Nations Convention on the Rights of the Child', *British Educational Research Journal*, 33, 6, 927–942.

Assesses some of the barriers to the meaningful and effective implementation of children's rights within education.

Van Krieken, R. (1999) 'The "stolen generations" and cultural genocide: the forced removal of Australian Indigenous children from their families and its implications for the sociology of childhood', *Childhood*, 6, 3, 297–311.

Discusses the atrocity of the Australian government's policy of forced separation of Aboriginal children from their birth families as part of an assimilation programme. Strikes at the very heart of children's fundamental human rights.

United Nations Convention on the Rights of the Child (1989) Geneva: United Nations. Also available online at www.everychildmatters.gov.uk/uncrc

Children's Rights Information Network www.crin.org [accessed 27/02/09].

The Relationship between the Researcher and the Researched

5

Chapter Outline

Introduction and key questions

Earlier in the book I outlined some of the critical issues around power dynamics and ethical considerations in research involving children. In this chapter I put the relationship between the researcher and the researched under the microscope and look at this from a practice perspective in four different types of research activity: research *on* children, research *about* children, research *with* children and research *by* children. Each type of research is examined through case study examples. I also look at the effect on research relationships of the context in which the research takes place, focusing on the environments of school, home and community. Issues of exploitation, adult filtering, cultural adjustments and mediated interpretations are addressed as they arise.

- Can the power held by adult researchers ever be considered abusive?
- How can adult researchers build rapport with child participants?

- Will I miss football if I stay and talk to you?
- Support versus management – how can we get the balance right?
- How does location and context affect the researcher–researched relationship?

Research *on* children

> ## Can the power held by adult researchers ever be considered abusive?

Power relations are at their most visible in research *on* children. Some would argue that the relationship between researchers and researched in some circumstances is nothing short of abusive, where adults use their absolute power over children to perpetrate cruel and damaging research *on* children. To illustrate this assertion, I have chosen to cite an example from the many twin studies that have been conducted over the years.

Research example: twins study

If you want to read the full story about this twins study, the twins have written it in their own words in a book entitled *Identical Strangers* (2007) by Elyse Schein and Paula Bernstein.

In the 1960s, identical twins were put up for adoption by their mother who was suffering with a mental illness. A famous New York psychologist, Viola Bernard, persuaded the adoption agency to separate the twins and send them to homes in different parts of New York, without telling the respective adoptive parents that each child had an identical twin. She and her co-investigator, Peter Neubauer, then secretly followed the twins' progress. They were primarily interested in whether identical twins would forge better individual identities if they were separated. Bernard wrote in 1963 that the study 'provides a natural laboratory situation for studying certain questions with respect to the nature-nurture issue and of family dynamic interactions in relation to personality development.' The study was never completed but one cubic foot of data was collected about the twins. On the death of Viola Bernard in 1998 the data were donated by the Child Development Center where she worked to Yale University. At the request of Peter Neubauer, the data boxes were sealed and will not be opened until 2020. It took the death of the principal researcher, Viola Bernard, for the revelation to come out – 35 years before Elyse and Paula were informed that they each had an identical twin.

Reflections on the research

Activity 1
What are your thoughts on the relationship between the researchers and the researched in this project?

Activity 2
Consider the following statements about the secret twin study. Do any of them resonate with you and if so, how strongly? What are your own views?

'To deliberately separate identical twins and to choose to prevent them from accessing their biological twin is not just unethical, it is child abusive.'

'The researchers put their needs before the needs of the twins.'

'Valuable knowledge about nature-nurture is generated from separated twin studies. Twins get separated all the time. It's no big deal.'

'The twins can never make up for 35 years that were lost to them, the study was cruel.'

'New knowledge is more important than ethical niceties.

Pause for thought

Some of the medical knowledge in our domain had its origins in the horrific experiments practised in Nazi concentration camps in the Second World War. Is it ethical to benefit from knowledge gained at the cost of so much human suffering (past) or is it unethical not to use that knowledge if it could prevent human suffering (present and future)? What do you think?

Of course not all research *on* children is an abuse of power and there have been some very fine studies that have informed our knowledge and understanding of children born as twins.

Research *about* children

> ## How can adult researchers build rapport with child participants?

In the stampede to privilege research *by* children, It would be foolhardy to overlook the very valuable research conducted by adults *about* children and childhoods. Here, the research relationship is about building rapport and trust because the researcher needs something from children and is not necessarily going to be giving anything back. So, although the power relations may not be as extreme as research *on* children, the needs–benefits scales are heavily tipped in favour of the adult researcher. Ethnographic approaches are common in this type of research. Building rapport is a crucial part of the research relationship. Adult researchers need to gain the trust and respect of the children. A child will be wary about disclosing information in an interview to someone they are afraid of, suspicious of or scornful of. Equally, children are unlikely to behave normally if they are being observed by someone they are afraid of, suspicious of or scornful of. An adult researcher does not have to become 'best buddies' with children in order to gain their trust, but mutual respect is essential. So, how might a researcher go about earning the respect of children? In the research example that follows, Sam Punch writes about her ethnographic study with children in rural Bolivia.

> ### Research example: children in rural Bolivia
>
> If you would like to read the full research report the reference is: Punch, S. (2004) 'Negotiating autonomy: children's use of time and space in rural Bolivia'. In Lewis, V. et al. (eds) *The Reality of Research with Children and Young People*, London: Sage in association with Open University Press.
>
>> Geographical isolation meant that both the children and adult participants had experienced limited contact with outsiders. Many children had never seen a white European before meeting me. At the start of the research they reacted with stares and nervous giggles. Living in the community and taking part in some of the participants' daily activities meant I could form a relationship of trust vital for gathering data . . .
>>
>> ⇨

Forming relationships of trust can take a long time and varies with different people. Some people never lost their suspicions of me as the foreign visitor to their community. Various signs indicated when I began to be more accepted such as when I was invited inside the house for the first time or when I was invited to eat a meal with household members rather than separately at the 'guest' table. Once, when a four year old girl was sitting on my lap, a neighbour warned the mother of the household to take her from me or one day I would steal her. Fortunately my relationship was sufficiently good with that household that they could laugh off her suggestions . . .

   Caution had to be taken never to promise to do something that I would not be able to fulfil, since many rural people have experienced disillusion with outsiders whose promises to improve their lives never materialised. . . . It took longer to form relationships of mutual trust with the children than with the adults because of the unequal power relationship between an adult researcher and a child participant. I spent time with these children: accompanying them on their daily tasks, playing with them, walking to school, observing their work, their songs, their games, and how they negotiated their relationships with their parents and siblings. Caution had to be taken over revealing the hidden aspects of children's lives to adults. If something was told in confidence I had to be careful not to mention it to their parents or teachers. For example, once I saw two children going fishing and they told me that they were supposed to be looking after their mother's cows. They asked me not to say anything to their mother if I saw her. Consequently, when I saw their mother and she asked if I had seen the children, I chose to lie and say I had not. (Punch, 2004, 99–100)

Reflections on the research

Activity 1
What can you glean about the relationship between researcher and researched from this extract? Think about building rapport, about trust and about making promises.

Activity 2
The quote below is from a commentary that Sam Punch wrote about her Bolivian study in which she gives an example of the cultural challenges of research relationships.

I tried to be sensitive to cultural distinctions but sometimes would make mistakes unknowingly. One such example of 'putting my foot in it' was on Christmas day when I was invited to celebrate with five-year-old Alma's family. I turned up with small gifts for the children but was surprised when they just stood happily clutching them unopened. They did not seem to know what to do with them, as they had never seen presents wrapped up before. Suddenly I felt awkward at being the rich *gringa* who could waste money on trivialities when the only Christmas presents they receive (if at all) is a new pair of shoes or a new hat.

Can you think of an example in your own or others' experience where a researcher might have had difficulty making similar cultural adjustments?

Cross (2002) in her comparative research with school children in Jamaica and Scotland writes about the value of relating to children in different contexts and that these alter the power relations between herself as a researcher and the children. Working in Jamaica, Cross discussed in depth how she approached her research:

> My analysis was one of negotiating and defining differences through play and work. Children's relative power within these activities was often highlighted by conflicts that arose during these activities. We did not discuss socio-economic theory; we did discuss its more relevant situated manifestation as experienced in bullying and school punishment. The terms of engagement were through popular icons, Bounty Killer not Giddens. (2002, 99)

Cross fully recognized the importance of the community of children she was operating in and the power relations this evoked.

Research *with* children

Will I miss football if I stay and talk to you?

In this next section I explore what conditions and characteristics constitute good relationships between researchers and researched where children participate in adult studies as participants or co-researchers. This espouses a position of researchers as co-learners in the enquiry process (Gramsci, 1971). Building rapport is just as important here as in the earlier ethnographic style of research *about* children. A first step is to be open and honest. Tell children who you are, what you are doing and why. Allow them to ask questions and answer these in an open and honest way. Do not deflect the difficult or awkward questions; ultimately children will respect a researcher far more for total honesty. For example if a researcher wants to do some focus group inter- views with children and one of them asks 'Will I miss football if I stay and talk to you?' the researcher has to be honest even if that risks losing a member from the focus group.

A particular distinctive form of participatory research with children has become known as PAR (Participatory Action Research) commonly applied in community settings to examine problems and promote change and involves several 'cycles' of action. It is a popular method with Non Governmental

Organizations (NGOs) and aims to involve children in the actual process of enquiry.

Research example: use of public space by street children

The research example I have chosen to illustrate PAR is a 3-year project involving street children in six different metropolitan districts of Turkey. The research study was investigating attitudes and approaches to the use of public space. The full reference is Ataov, A. and Haider, J. (2006) 'From participation to empowerment: critical reflections on a participatory action research project with street children in Turkey', *Children Youth and Environments*, 16, 2, 127–152.

> This project attempted to explore what constitutes effective participation and how PAR can empower street children as actors . . . it was about creating an understanding of the plight of street children with regard to public space in order to enable children to take collective action to empower themselves. This perspective is vital for children's empowerment because adults and professionals have a tendency to mold children into adults' way of thinking about the environment – an attitude that prevents meaningful dialogue or grasp of the democratic use of public space by all stakeholders. . . . By applying a PAR approach, this study was aimed at enabling children to develop new local knowledge combined with practice. The process concentrated on empowering children and creating a learning environment in which children could systematize their real-life situations, formulate the best solutions to address their problems, and act upon their decisions. . . . Having different tasks and responsibilities, the research and coordinating team, field practitioners, and street children shared and collectively generated all methodological and analytical knowledge . . .
>
> Practitioners engaged with children through a process of understanding their life stories and their present conditions, and formulating action plans to ameliorate their current state. . . . Once the feedback from children was retrieved, practitioners and the coordinating team would re-gather for reflection, which would be discussed with children again, and so the research cycle continued. . . . To convey their living and working conditions on the street, children engaged in a number of participatory activities. Under the moderation of social workers, children used art as a medium to communicate their perceptions of the street, their experiences, their likes and dislikes. Children drew cognitive maps of their experiences on the street. They produced graphics of their support network. They enacted dramas to present their relations with other children, social workers, policemen, shopkeepers, and local municipal inspectors on the street. They created maps of their migration within the country, including their origin, destination, duration of stay in a city, and migration intervals. By taking pictures and interviewing other peers, children revealed their self-perception in the media and indicated how they would like to be known by the general public. At the end of each art activity, children collectively discussed what they meant by the way they drew, played, and photographed. Finally, children engaged in in-depth discussions about their life stories. (pp. 132–137)

Reflections on the research

Activity

Think about the ways in which the street children were actively involved in this research. Did the choice of data generation tools enable their participation to be more meaningful? Was this partnership between adults and children an empowering experience?

Key points

- There is no researcher–researched relationship in research *on* children as children are merely the objects of research.
- Sometimes the researcher's role towards children can be exploitative – occasionally even abusive.
- Research *about* children requires a rapport between researcher and researched in order to build trust and mediate power relations especially where there are cultural difference. This enhances the prospect of more accurate naturalistic data which is not contaminated by participants' eagerness to please or suspicion/fear of the researcher.
- PAR is a form of participatory action research where the research relationship between children and adults is a partnership in which they work together on a community issue.

Research *by* children

Support versus management – how can we get the balance right?

When we consider research undertaken by children themselves, we are looking at two kinds of relationship: firstly the relationship between child researcher and adult supporter and secondly the relationship between child researcher and child participant.

The first of these is very different from any of the adult–child research relationships we have looked at so far in this chapter. The adult role is to

Table 2 Getting the balance right

Getting the balance right	
support	management
enabling: promoting the idea that children can undertake their own research	influencing: allowing adult interest/agendas to influence what children research
sustaining: training children in research process including data collection and analysis methods	limiting: only teaching children certain skills thereby reducing their ability to make informed choices
supporting: paving the way for children with gatekeepers	judging: suggesting that a child's idea is not worthy enough to research
helping: helping children with some of the leg work rather than the design work e.g. transcribing interviews, number crunching, report writing frameworks	controlling: controlling access to participants e.g. in a school not allowing children to observe or interview certain peer groups or staff
empowering: actively seeking dissemination platforms for child researchers	hijacking: hijacking the content of children's research and/or the ownership of the research

support the child researchers, not to control or manage them. It is an empowering process that negotiates access with gatekeepers and provides training and resources, not one that closes down options or imposes adult norms. Getting the balance right is not easy as is demonstrated in Table 2.

Neither is it always easy for children to relate to adults in this way when they are conditioned to seeing adults in authoritarian roles. Even after working with children for several weeks and having asked them to call me by my first name from the outset, they frequently revert to the 'Miss' labelling. This is a particular issue when working with children in school contexts.

The relationship between child researcher and child participant is new territory and some positioning still needs to be worked out here. The aim is for power relations to be neutral in child–child interactions, especially when collecting data. But this is not always the case. There are many sets of circumstances where power dynamics are at work, not unduly dissimilar to society at large:

- Older children with younger children
- Popular with less popular children
- Articulate with less articulate children
- Rich children with poor children
- Children deemed to have an 'official status' such as prefect, sports captain, club leader, etc. with children who have none.

- Typically developing children with children who have a learning disability
- Able-bodied children with disabled children.

And it works both ways. It is not always the child researcher who is in the position of power. Some child researchers feel overawed at the thought of interviewing an older or a more popular child, of being ridiculed as a 'geek' or the subject of jealousy that they have been given 'research privileges'. Research relations need to be addressed as part of the training of child researchers, exploring how potential power relations can be neutralized. What we are most concerned to avoid is a replication of the much criticized mediated adult researcher accounts of children's experiences being recreated in mediated child researcher accounts. The power of child–child research should be that it transcends these power dynamics and propagates authentic insider perspectives. The next research example is by two 10-year-old researchers and typifies how power relations can be mitigated when data is collected child–child.

Research example: child–child research relationship

Ruth Forrest and Naomi Dent (2003) are two 10-year-old researchers investigating how 9-to 11-year-old children are affected by the nature of their parents' jobs. You can read their full report on the Children's Research Centre website at http://child-rens-research-centre.open.ac.uk [accessed 24/01/09]

> We were interested in how parent's jobs affect their children and wondered how children are affected by the kind of hours parents work and the sorts of moods they come home in, for instance if they come home very tired or angry or if they come home happy and bouncy. How does this affect the quality of relationships in the family?

Ruth and Naomi were researching this topic with their peers and wanted to be able to get their peers to tell them what they really felt about their parents' jobs without any adult pressure. As part of their research they created a number of statements and asked participants to say how strongly or otherwise they agreed with them. The statements were in language they thought their peers would identify with. Here are some of Ruth and Naomi's statements from their questionnaire.

> 'How much do you think your parents enjoy their jobs?'
> 'Do you think the hours your parents work are . . .?'
> 'My parent's job gets in the way of them playing with me'.
> 'My parents' work gets in the way of coming to school events'.
> 'Which is your favourite day of the week with your parent(s)?'

Figures 3 and 4 show some examples of their analyzed data.

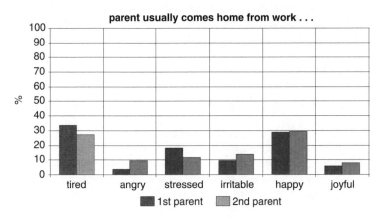

Figure 3 'My parent usually comes home from work . . .'

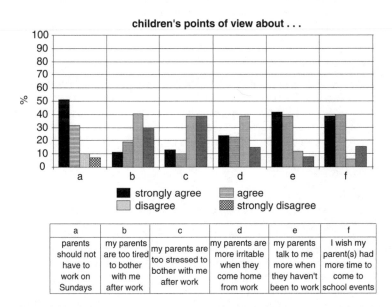

a	b	c	d	e	f
parents should not have to work on Sundays	my parents are too tired to bother with me after work	my parents are too stressed to bother with me after work	my parents are more irritable when they come home from work	my parents talk to me more when they haven't been to work	I wish my parent(s) had more time to come to school events

Figure 4 Children's points of view about their parents' work

Reflections on the research

Activity 1

Think about the language that Ruth and Naomi have used and whether this is different from language adults might have used. For example in Figure 3 the word 'joyful' appears as one category choice to describe how children think a parent feels at the end of a working day. Joyful is not a word that would spring to most adult minds! But why should children not conceive of their parents finding work 'joyful'?

This is what the two young researchers concluded.

> We were quite surprised that most children seemed to be quite content about their parents' jobs. We hear a lot about the stress of people's jobs and how this affects the family but this didn't seem to be the case in our investigation. . . . Although angry, stressed and irritable were lower scores, it's interesting that more mums seem to come home angry and irritable than dads but more dads come home stressed. But approximately a third of parents came home 'tired' and a third came home 'happy' so it seems that the majority of children in Years 5 and 6 at our school think their parents come home happy but tired rather than angry and stressed. . . . Contrary to our predictions, it seemed that most children thought their parents enjoyed their jobs quite a lot and that the hours they worked were 'just right'. Although children 'wished' that parents could have more time to come to their school events they didn't seem to mind too much and the fact that they didn't feel strongly about this suggests that perhaps they are realistic about the situation and accept it.

Activity 2

Before they began their research Ruth and Naomi hypothesized that children of their age would probably feel resentful about their parents' jobs but this did not prove to be the case. They did not let their own hunch bias their research design and were very honest in reporting the findings even though they were not what they expected. Do you think it is harder for children or adults to accept that a hypothesis is wrong? Do you think the presence of a hypothesis changes the dynamics between researcher and researched?

Activity 3

Never quite willing to let go of their original hypothesis, Ruth and Naomi explored the same theme with a 6-year-old girl.

> Interestingly when we tried out our questionnaire on a six-year-old her thoughts were very different compared to the 10 and 11-year-olds. She wanted her mum and dad to be at school events much more and to play with her more at home.

If Ruth and Naomi were to investigate this with 6-year-olds on a larger scale, what do you think they would have to consider to ensure their study was unbiased and free from any power dynamics?

How does location and context affect the researcher–researched relationship?

In this section I examine the effect of location and context on relationships between the researcher and the researched. Three locations are considered: school, home and community.

The school environment

Children in Western societies spend a large proportion of their childhood at school and a substantial amount of child research is undertaken in school contexts. I have already alluded in Chapter 2 to some of the acute power relations that are present. Here, I look in more depth at the effect of this on research relationships. It is quite common for teachers to undertake action research in their classrooms. This presents several challenges – not least the tension in the dual role of researcher and teacher.

Research example: researcher–researched relationships

A teacher in a primary school was interested in using Information and Communication Technology (ICT) more effectively and particularly wanted to help reluctant writers in literacy lessons. He designed a writing frame as a computer programme with word banks, word prompts and other tools to help the reluctant writer. He piloted this with one of his classes for half a term and then decided to evaluate how effective it had been. His main method of evaluation was interviewing the children. While the findings were very positive and the children appeared to like using the computer programme, it does raise some interesting questions.

Reflections on the research

Activity
Reflect on these questions:

- How honest do you think children would be when asked by a teacher if they liked a teacher's innovation?
- Do you think this invalidates the findings in any way?
- This comes under the jurisdiction of curriculum; would it have been possible for any children to dissent from participating even if he or she had wanted to?
- It is an important aspect of learning for a teacher to want to investigate – can you think of ways he might have gone about this that would have altered the researcher–researched relationship?

Home environment

Researcher–researched relationships can be different in home compared to school environments.

Activity

Suppose you want to explore what role humour plays in sibling relationships in the home compared to humour in school friendships. Do you think your relationship as researcher would be different in the home environment compared to school environment? If so, in what ways?

Community environment

The next research example looks at the research relationship with very young children in a community setting and is an excellent vehicle for exploring a number of issues that arise in research relations where there is a large age disparity.

Research example: adult researcher–young child relationship

In a study entitled '"Don't come too close to my octopus tree": Recording and evaluating young children's perspectives on outdoor learning' (Waller, T., 2006, *Children Youth and Environments*, 16, 2, 75–104) the researcher explored 3-and 4-year-olds' responses to the outdoor play area of a local country park over a period of 7 months. He wanted to privilege the children's perspectives and had to be particularly careful to nullify power relationships because of the young ages of the participants. He drew on the work of Clark and Moss (2001 and 2005) and Chawla (2002) to develop participatory methods that would allow the data to unfold through the children themselves. Clark and Moss developed a participatory research method for young children known as the 'mosaic approach'. This uses a range of tools such as children taking photographs, taking adults on guided tours of their worlds, drawing maps and pictures, group chats alongside the adult researcher's own observations and listening, 'The mosaic approach enables children to create a living picture of their lives' (Clark and Moss, 2005, 13).

The country park used in Waller's study is built around an Edwardian reservoir and arboretum and has the appeal of a natural, wild environment. It includes an area of 52,000 square metres of woods, open grassland, a children's play area, a pond and a butterfly park.

Data collection starts with children using digital photographs and film to record their perspectives. The children are asked to tell a story of their visit by taking photos of their favourite places ('happy' places and 'special' places) that then become a starting point for discussion with an adult. The child and a practitioner discuss the child's photograph as a representation of the child's interest, play or activity, and the discussion is then recorded as a 'learning story'. . . . In addition some children have been encouraged to photograph a tour for a 'new visitor'.

. . . *Ben's story*

Ben asked to use the video camera; he picked it up and turned it on. He then walked up the path past a large open meadow.

I am trying to find dinosaurs. Ssh Ssh. You have to be very quiet.

That looks like where I play football with Mathew – he's my older brother.

He then walked up the path towards the woods.

You have to be very quiet to look for dinosaurs.

After several minutes of filming, Ben put the camera down on the ground.

This camera is too heavy now.

. . . Ben looked through the viewfinder of the video camera.

See here it's fantastic, you can see them right over there. Look – it's pointing that way.

He put the camera down again and picked up his stick.

This is to beat dinosaurs up with. Found some nearby dinosaurs.

Ben ran off into the woods waving his stick in the air.

Ssh. Only I can talk!'

. . . In much participatory research, adult control over children's engagement in the research process represents a dilemma of power. However . . . what occurs in children's spaces is defined by the ethos and style of interaction between adults and children. . . . Rather than thinking about engaging children's views simply to influence planning and design (and the corresponding danger of instrumentalizing children's play), we need to rethink participation in terms of 'spaces for childhood' within which children can exercise their agency to participate in their own decisions, actions and meaning-making, which may or may not involve engagement with adults . . . staff are reflective practitioners, thinkers, researchers and co-constructors of knowledge with children. (pp. 83–95)

Reflections on the research

Activity
How would you describe the relationship between this adult researcher and the very young child participants in his study? Think about what the power dynamics might be? Do you think this offers a genuine way in which very young children can participate in research about matters that affect their lives such as their play spaces?

Interview with Sue Bucknall about research relationships

Sue Bucknall is Research Associate, Children's Research Centre, Open University, UK, and former primary school teacher.

Mary: What are your views about power dynamics in adult–child researcher–participant relationships?

Sue: It's great that the movement towards decreasing power differentials in this context is gaining momentum but I think the issue is certainly not straightforward because there are so many other factors that impinge on research relations above and beyond the researcher and the participant. For instance, if I think about my own experiences of carrying out research with children and young people – which have all taken place in school environments – I know that the context in which the research takes place impacts heavily on the relationships I have had with participants because of the power dynamics which already exist there. Maybe my own role as a facilitator for the Children's Research Centre positions me 'differently' on this issue as my work is geared heavily towards empowering children to have a greater say and be listened to by adults and towards trying to balance the power relations between us when I am supporting their research. I've certainly always been aware how switching roles from facilitator to being a researcher with children as my participants creates some tensions! It sometimes isn't enough to try to balance power relations in these situations as best I can (for example by using methods which encourage the children's active participation and which respect the ways they like to communicate) because, as an adult researcher, I have some-times been effectively (although I don't think deliberately) disempow-ered by other adults and my plans reduced to ashes!

I say 'try' to reduce the unequal power relationship because I don't think it is possible to remove this from the equation altogether – again, I think this is especially so when carrying out research in schools, because children and young people are so used to the adults 'being in charge' and I think it must be difficult for them to adapt their ways of being in school when they work with a researcher particularly when this is a 'one-off' event. For example, I've found it particularly interesting when I have been into schools to facilitate focus groups with children who have become 'young researchers' and, separately, with their peers (who have not). These young researchers have been used to working with adults external to the school in ways that are 'different' to their usual school experiences and have been much easier to engage in focus group activities on a more equal footing – even making suggestions about how certain activities could be improved so that they could be more effective in conveying the children's own views. For example, two groups of young researchers in two separate focus groups were asked to rank child-generated statements (taken from earlier interviews with other groups) in order to show what they thought was the most important thing about becoming a young researcher in a primary school. Both groups happily completed the activity but pointed out that these were not necessarily the things they would have said. The children then wrote their own statements and, with their agreement, the activity was repeated a couple of weeks later using the new statements.

This eagerness to work *with* me in this way was not apparent in the groups of the young researchers' peers where I felt the children were happily engaged but, nevertheless, working *for* me. Perhaps this raises the issue of whether or not children and young people need to be 'skilled up' in order to be able to engage with adults on a more equal footing – for the majority, this is unchartered water. Children I have talked to about their experiences of becoming researchers have attested to feeling more adult, or more like equals and feeling in control because of the ways in which relationships between themselves and their adult facilitators were allowed to develop.

I think another thing that might be school-specific is the difficulty that arises when teachers choose the groups who are to be participants in a study. Despite attending to all the issues and choices involved in gaining the children's informed consent I think it is hard for children to say 'no' to an adult – and perhaps even harder to say 'no' to a visitor in school than to a teacher. I don't know what can be done about this. Trying to engage with children in ways that reduce power differentials between us certainly challenges existing structures in schools. Perhaps the new legislation making it a legal requirement for schools to listen to pupils' voices might make some difference – it will be interesting to see if this really has an effect on school culture and, subsequently, on the ways adult researchers can work with child participants in this context. If children do not have the necessary experience or competences to engage with adults on a more equal basis the dangers of them second-guessing the 'required' responses (perhaps relating to their experiences in the classroom) are always present: 'Well, what do you want me to answer?', said one 11-year-old I was interviewing.

Mary: The child–child researcher–participant relationship is becoming more common, what are the critical issues in this emerging role?

Sue: Well, first of all, I think it is dangerous to assume that if children and young people are carrying out research with children then this solves the problems associated with adult–child participant power relations. My experience of working with children as young researchers has raised my awareness that power dynamics can still be problematic for them during the course of their research – they are just different power relations and can be problematic in different ways although sometimes the same problems arise. The 'please the adult' phenomenon, for example, is a recognized element in adult-to-child research but this can be translated to 'please my friend' when children are carrying out research with their peers. Conversely, children can exercise power in more deliberately negative ways by being silly or disruptive in interviews or writing silly answers in questionnaires, for example. Young researchers I have talked with have found this hard to deal with and usually attribute it to social relationships between them and their peers.

So, I think another important thing to bear in mind is that children are not a homogeneous group. Differences in gender, ethnicity, age, class and mental/physical ability/disability all exist and children are well aware of the differences between them and how these can impact on power relations. In some schools where it isn't 'cool to be clever' but the school has selected a group of more able children to form the school's research group, it is not unusual for these children to have to cope with being seen as a 'boff' or a 'geek' and this can make them reluctant to pursue data collection in ways that demonstrate their abilities. Interestingly, this seems to be less of a problem in secondary schools than in primaries. However, there is another issue here and that is the difficulty able children sometimes have in engaging their peers during research projects in ways that allow less able children to respond effectively. Young researchers, too, need to be 'child-friendly'! Adult research with children is often criticized on the grounds that adult researchers bring with them their own interests and pre-assumptions, especially about issues they consider to be important – but in my experience children are just as likely to do this! In fact, young researchers have often told me that one of the main things they have been most surprised about during their research experience has been discovering that other pupils or students do not feel the same way about issues as they do.

That said, the upside is that generally children are much more likely than adults to be aware of how children like to communicate and how they use language so can carry out their research in ways that adults can't. They also understand issues in different ways – I remember in one school a young researcher wanted to investigate bullying but was told that there was 'no bullying' in his school. His research revealed that verbal bullying was (as he suspected) more prevalent than was realized by staff – perhaps not surprising in view of the school's tough policy towards dealing with physical bullying. As a result of his research, the school's bullying policy was revised.

Children have told me that they are usually more willing to talk to other children about some issues because they feel their responses are less likely to be judged – and that they don't feel they have to guess the 'right' answer. This speaks very strongly to issues of power and to the nature of the data that can be collected.

Mary: To what extent does the topic being researched affect the researcher–researched relationship and do you have any examples you can share with me?

Sue: Two things come immediately to mind here. The first is that while children can, as I've just said, be more willing to talk to young researchers, they have also told me that in some instances they would feel more comfortable talking with an adult about some issues because they can trust the adult to treat what they tell them as confidential. They are not, it seems, always willing to trust their peers to do this (despite confidentiality and anonymity being discussed and agreed on) and so this inevitably affects the researcher–researched relationship in so far as what can be talked about. So trust and the sensitivity of the topic is enormously important.

The second returns to schools as contexts for research. I'm thinking of one particular school where students were investigating issues relating to teaching and learning. One topic was the use of practical activities in lessons and the students wanted to carry out lesson observations. It was not surprising that difficulties were encountered since (as one teacher I interviewed told me) some teachers saw this as a threat and a direct challenge to their normal classroom practice. However, as the school leadership team were keen for this research to go ahead, some members of staff felt they had no choice but to consent to the observations so relations were, in some instances, at best rather unhappy – an interesting example of how power circulates in schools. In my experience, pupils and students can be reluctant to investigate teaching and learning issues, suspecting that this might result in negative fallout for them. This, of course, brings us back to school culture and I know that in many schools now, where the voices of both students *and* staff are listened to and respected, teachers and students do work alongside or with each other to investigate these issues successfully.

Key points

- When adults empower children to research in their own right care has to be taken to get the balance right between *supporting* children's research and *managing* it.
- Research *by* children generally minimizes the kind of power dynamics that can beleaguer adult–child research. But power considerations still do exist and can manifest themselves in child–child research where there are e.g. age, race, cognitive and popularity issues.
- Location and context can have a significant impact on the researcher–researched relationship especially if there are power dynamics in the environment. School locations are particularly predisposed to reinforce adult–child power and this needs to be factored in to any research undertaken in schools.

Summary

This chapter has:

- Looked at the relationship between adult researcher and child subject in research studies *on* children and the acute power dynamics involved.
- Explored the difficulties of building rapport and trust in research relationships between adults and children in research studies *about* childhood.
- Considered participation as a primary factor in research *with* children.
- Challenged some of the 'fluffy' thinking around research relationships in research *by* children, particularly the notion that power relations are not an issue.
- Examined the researcher–researched relationship in different types of research.
- Reviewed research that raises different types of researcher–researched relationships in order to relate the issues to real world situations.

Suggested further reading

Griesel, D., Swart-Kruger, J. and Chawla, L. (2004) 'Children in South Africa can make a difference: an assessment of "Growing Up in Cities" in Johannesburg'. In Fraser, S. et al. (eds) *The Reality of Research with Children and Young People*, London: Sage in association with Open University Press, pp. 277–295.

This is an account of a PAR project in Johannesburg where children were actively involved in transformative action for their communities.

Gallagher, M. (2009) 'Researching the geography of power in a primary school'. In Tisdall, K., Davis, J. and Gallagher, M. (eds) *Researching with Children and Young People: Research Design, Methods and Analysis*, London: Sage, pp. 57–64.

This case study reflects on the role of the researcher in a Primary classroom and has a particularly good discussion around the ethical dilemmas of informed consent.

Hill, M. (2005) 'Ethical considerations in researching children's experiences'. In Greene, S. and Hogan, D. (eds) *Researching Children's Experience*, London: Sage, pp. 61–86.

This chapter debates many of the ethical issues that can affect the research-researched relationship.

6

Children and Young People as Researchers

Introduction and key questions

A book that invites a rethinking of children and research cannot be complete without a section devoted to the most recent and contemporary of attitudinal shifts: children undertaking and leading their own research. Within this paradigm, children set their own research agendas, explore issues about their lives which they, rather than adults, determine are important and research them from their perspectives. There is no suggestion that research by children will, or should, replace adult-led child research, rather that the two exist as complementarities. Research by children offers a nuanced insider perspective of a relatively powerless minority group and shares some congruence with early developments in feminist and disability research. This chapter focuses exclusively on research *by* children.

- Why is it important that children undertake their own research?
- How young can children engage in their own research?
- Are children in other parts of the world doing their own research?
- Can research by children and young people inform policy?

Why is it important that children undertake their own research?

Children observe with different eyes, ask different questions – they sometimes ask questions that adults do not even think of – have different concerns and immediate access to a peer culture where adults are outsiders. The research agendas children prioritize, the research questions they frame and the way in which they collect data are also quintessentially different from adults. Child–child research generates nuanced data which provide valuable insights into our understanding of childhoods. This is unlike some of the other kinds of research discussed in this book and it is important to distinguish this from children as participatory or co-researchers. While there are some obvious benefits in children designing and leading their own research in that this gets closer to children's lived experiences and illuminates their insider perspective, there are also some challenges. Most children need adult support to be able to carry out their own research and this can be time consuming and costly. It also presents some barriers.

A principal barrier to children undertaking their own research is their lack of research knowledge and skills. Many adults also lack these skills and could not carry out quality research without some training so notions of the barriers being a within-child deficit do not stand up to close scrutiny. The Children's Research Centre (CRC) at the Open University, UK, focuses on optimal ways to develop children's research knowledge and skills and support children to undertake their own research. The CRC aims to minimize adult filters by shifting the balance to *supporting* rather than *managing* children's research (see http://childrens-research-centre.open.ac.uk [accessed 24/01/09]).

The CRC offers diverse groups of children a taught programme of research process followed by assistance to carry out research projects about aspects of their lives that concern or interest them. The centre supports a variety of outreach programmes with links to schools and community organizations. At the time of writing, its website is host to over a hundred research studies by children and young people.

Some children undertake social research about issues that preoccupy adult researchers and policy makers e.g. racial discrimination, poverty, bullying, social exclusion, educational attainment, knife crime, etc. It is an opportunity for adults to access evidence-based child perspectives from within children's peer culture and inform our knowledge and understanding about challenging issues. There is also a growing body of research by children and young people from around the world, including majority world countries.

Research example: East meets West

To illustrate this point, I have chosen a study exploring the difficulties of 'double identity' facing many second and third generation immigrant populations as they struggle to cope with cultural and religious ideologies that conflict with modern youth in British society. The research was carried out by a group of South Asian young people exploring how cultural and religious issues affect them and in particular why they feel they need to lead a double identity. The young researchers were S. Ahmad, A. Akbar, H. Akbar, S. Ayub, A. Batool, S. Battol, B. Hussain, S. Kiani, S. Mahmood and R. Rauf. The research was supported by Barnardos and the Young Researcher Network (run by the National Youth Agency). You can find the full report at www.nya.org.uk/youngresearchernetwork or at http://childrens-research-centre. open.ac.uk [accessed 24/01/09]. It was published in 2009.

The young people collected three sets of data:

- Focus group (with 6 young people)
- One-to-one interviews (with 8 young people, 5 parents and 3 professionals)
- Questionnaire (n = 35)

Here are some of their findings (pp. 27–33):

- Peer pressure, parental pressure and media pressure were identified as strong factors in their leading double identity lives.
- 66 per cent stated they led a double identity but could not speak to their families about this.
- 30 per cent of participants felt they were trapped between their culture/ethnicity and the modern Western society they live in.
- 34 per cent behave differently at home compared to other environments.
- 55 per cent identified that they felt judged and needed to lead a double identity in order to fit in, particular reasons were: skin colour; appearance; dress code; culture and religion.

Examples of double identity behaviour included hiding mobile phones from parents, wearing different clothes outside the home but changing before returning home, keeping friendships with boys concealed and secret smoking.

At the end of their study, the young researchers made some recommendations:

- Better education for professionals on cultural and religious issues and needs;
- Better specialist services to meet the health and emotional wellbeing needs of South Asian young people;
- Involvement of young people from Asian communities in the planning and implementation of appropriate specialist services from the outset;
- Professionals from schools, education, health and social services need to understand how ideas of parenting, childhood and 'youth' differ not only between ethnic groups but also within each sub ethnic group.

Reflections on the research

Activity 1

The following quotes are taken from the focus group and individual interviews (pp. 20–26). What themes can you ascertain from the young people's own words about double identity issues?

- 'My parents are very religious and they don't let me wear English clothes but my mates all tell me to wear English clothes'.
- 'A person could be pressured by friends, and it can be hard to say no as you don't want to be left out'.
- 'When you watch TV it makes you think differently'.
- 'They feel embarrassed [wearing a headscarf] on the streets, they want to look like their friends'.
- 'We are not allowed to go out. When me and my boyfriend 'Mayah' (I call him a girl's name because my mum would get suspicious) real name Harron meet, I say I am going to school'.
- 'My parents tell me to pray every day five times a day but I don't want to'.
- 'It is difficult to say no to friends because they then start back biting so you follow because you don't want that, you want to be like every body else'.
- 'If I spike my hair my parents think I hang around with the wrong crowd'.
- 'They call Pakistani girls sluts if they wear short sleeves'.
- 'Sometimes a person can feel trapped and does not have a choice but to listen to family due to cultural reasons and therefore has no freedom'.
- 'I never listen to my parents they don't know I talk to boys if they did know they would kill me'.
- 'Only Muslim friends [are allowed home] because they might not do nasty stuff like non Muslims'.
- 'You could be forced into smoking, boyfriends and stuff when you don't want to'.
- 'Friends might force you to do something against your religion and culture'.

- 'I do it because our parents are happy when we wear it [a headscarf], but my friends are white and they don't get why I wear it'.
- 'My friends they have never come to my house'.
- 'People comment on your clothes, hair, etc. which can put your confidence down'.
- 'My mum complains to me whenever I wear English clothes she says "what if my friends saw you what would they say?"'

Activity 2

Reflect on what young people as researchers bring to this study? Could the same data have been generated by adults?

Key points

- Children view the world differently from adults and can offer a different research perspective.
- Children's perspectives on their worlds are not easy for adults, as outsiders, to access.
- Arguments that children are not competent enough to undertake their own research have been robustly challenged.
- Research by children and young people is valuable and worthy of attention.

How young can children engage in their own research?

This is a frequently asked question and a very important one. There are several issues to consider. First of all we need to understand what is meant by research and how this is distinct from general enquiry and from school projects. The most common forms of enquiry, particularly with young children, involve secondary data: searching and sorting information to find an answer to a question e.g. what is the capital of Pakistan? How many litres of water does it take to fill a paddling pool? Here there is a known answer which children set out to discover. School projects are often an open-ended collection of enquiries around a theme e.g. a school project on the Rain Forest, the Tudors or nutritional content in foodstuffs. Curriculum-based projects might sometimes have an element of data generation in them. For example if a group of pupils decided to do a traffic survey as part of a geography project they would be creating some new data in the process. Another example might be a child interviewing old people about their wartime experiences. So where do we draw the line between research and enquiry?

Enquiry is one research skill, collecting data is another research skill, neither constitutes an empirical research study in its own right. An empirical research study is a process not an entity and there are several parts to the process. This starts with designing an ethical study, choosing appropriate data generation methods (which pre-supposes knowledge of a range of research methods in order to make this an informed choice), reasoned analysis, positioning of the findings in a context and the dissemination of outcomes. These require a certain level of stamina, competency and social maturity not normally associated with very young children. There will always be some exceptions and I am sure there are 5-year-olds who could manage to do this (just as there are some children who can achieve a maths degree by the age of 11) but they are relatively rare individuals. While acknowledging the possible, I would like to focus on the probable. Supporting very young children (aged 3–6 years) to engage in research is about introducing them to *some* of the processes and developing *some* of their embryonic research skills rather than getting them to undertake a whole empirical study. Young children have fascinating ideas, generate interesting enquiries, can carry out some simple data collection and produce some simple findings. These and any other activities which develop research skills are to be encouraged from an early age especially activities which develop lateral, imaginative and creative thinking.

Pause for thought

There is much good practice being realized around the world that stimulates and develops embryonic research skills with young children. Developing questioning is a really good starting point. Here are two thoughtful questions from young children at a school in Latvia.

> 'What happens to the soul of the frog when it dies?'
> 'How does the rooster know when to crow in the mornings?'
> (http://projekt.hib.no/caripsie[accessed 03/02/09])

Getting involved in research activity from an early age is also to be encouraged. Clark and Moss's (2001) very successful mosaic approach has led the way in participatory research methods with young children. Their focus is on listening to young children and facilitating their participation in research activity in partnership with adults. This builds important frameworks and develops skills which young children can use when they become active researchers in later years.

How young? Evidence shows that 9-year-olds have coped well with whole small scale research projects if appropriately supported by adults (Kellett, 2005). There is every reason to explore possibilities with younger children. This is still a relatively blank canvas and it is likely to be another decade before we have enough evidence to evaluate the exciting possibilities. To be meaningful for children, particularly young children, research undertaken must emanate from their own experience, be very small scale and involve simple analysis techniques. The next research example demonstrates these principles.

Research example: a small-scale study by a 10-year-old boy

Christopher Orme, aged 10, carried out some research in his school and local community about views and perceptions of the Police. He was part of a group of children in a primary school in Milton Keynes who were trained in research methods by university research staff. Christopher disseminated his findings as a PowerPoint presentation (see Orme, 2008, http://childrens-research-centre.open.ac.uk [accessed 24/01/09]). He separated his data into adults' and children's views so that he could compare them. There were some surprising results. 'Before I started this research project I thought that people did not like the Police so I am a little bit surprised that most people like them' (slide 32). Christopher produced some simple graphs from his questionnaire data. These indicated that more children than adults thought the Police helped people but adults scored higher than children on being happy that the Police were around in the community. Christopher compared what adults and children thought the Police did on the street – the categories he gave them to rank were:

- protecting streets from vandalism
- helping people
- making sure everybody is alright
- stopping bullying
- looking to see if people are doing crime
- protecting the community
- making friends
- preventing litter throwing
- stopping people from stealing
- arresting people
- doing their job
- solving crime
- looking out for fights

- looking for safe driving
- questioning people
- noticing changes
- as a deterrent
- making notes
- scaring me
- making me feel safe
- helping people who are lost
- understanding problems in the community

Figures 5 and 6 show examples of how he presented some of his findings in his PowerPoint presentation (slides 16 and 18 of 35).

What do you think the police do when they're out on the streets?

Top 5 things suggested by 7- to 18-year-olds
- Protecting the community
- Looking to see if the people are doing crime
- Making sure that everybody is alright
- Helping people
- (Joint 5th)
  - ○ Protecting streets from vandalism
  - ○ Arresting people

What do you think the police do when they're out on the streets?

Top 5 things suggested by 7-18 YEAR olds:
- Protecting the community
- Looking to see if the people are doing crime
- Making sure that everybody is alright
- Helping people
- (Joint 5th)

○ Protecting streets from vandalism
○ Arresting people

Figure 5 Children's perceptions (source: Orme (2008) http://childrens-research-centre.open.ac.uk)

What do you think the police do when they're out on the streets?

Top 5 things suggested by 19-year-olds and over

- Looking to see if people are doing crime
- As a deterrent – this means the police being around stops people from doing crime
- (Joint 3rd)
  - Protecting the community
  - Making friends
  - Making me feel safe

What do you think the police do when they're out on the streets?

Top 5 things suggested by 19 and over:

- Looking to see if the people are doing crime
- As a deterrent – this means the police being around stops people from doing crime

- (Joint 3rd)
  - Protecting the community
  - Making friends
  - Making me feel safe

Figure 6 Adult perceptions (source: Orme (2008) http://childrens-research-centre. open.ac.uk)

After Christopher had collected his questionnaire data he interviewed a police community officer to get her views on what a typical day on the beat is like. When he pulled all of this together, Christopher was able to compare public (child and adult) perceptions of local policing with what actually happened and found a lot of congruence. This also surprised him because he had expected to find more negative reactions to the police because of stereotyping in the media. Christopher found it interesting to explore where the perceptions of the Police differed between adults and children (and also where they were similar).

The simplicity of Christopher's research belies its poignancy. There was a degree of synergy in adult and children's top 3 judgements about what they thought the Police did on the streets (see Figures 5 and 6). However, the view of a policeman keeping you safe and making friends appeared near the top of adult perceptions but was almost non-existent on children's barometers. The reverse was true of the category of the Police 'scaring me' which did not figure in adult views but was evident in children's data. So even such a small project as this one by a 10-year-old boy, can make some valid points. Here they are about the perception of the 'public face' of the local Police. Christopher's data suggests that it is adults not children who see Police as 'making friends', and adults not children who are volunteering that Police make them 'feel safe' when visible in the community. His research has raised awareness that some confidence-building measures might be needed to try and present a friendlier Police face to the children in that community.

Reflections on the research

Activity

Think about possible benefits of children of Christopher's age doing small research projects that explore community issues from children's perspectives. Why might they produce different data from adult studies?

Pause for thought

By keeping his research small-scale, Christopher was able to complete all aspects of his study from design to dissemination. It is too small a study to make any generalizations from, and this was neither the intention nor the goal. Its value is in providing a small, cultural snapshot of how the Police are viewed by close members of his local community. If small research projects like this were being carried out by large numbers of children in large numbers of locations, this would create multiple cultural snapshots and soon build into a rich canvas of knowledge about children's perceptions on our world.

Key points

- We need to distinguish between empirical research and general enquiry/school projects.
- Activities which develop research skills are to be encouraged from an early age especially activities which develop lateral, imaginative and creative thinking.
- Research undertaken by children is more meaningful if it emanates from their own experience.

Are children in other parts of the world doing their own research?

It is pleasing to see that a global focus on children's rights is resulting in a gradual increase in research activity by children around the world. A few examples include:

- A seven-European country project known as CARIPSIE (Children as researchers in primary schools in Europe) which ran for 3 years until early 2009 and piloted a system of children doing their own research as part of their school curriculum.
- Hungary, where children have a choice of seven national curriculums, one of the seven curriculums has research methods as a core element. Over 50 schools in Hungary have chosen this option.
- Cyprus, where a recent bi-communal project brought together Greek-Cypriot and Turkish-Cypriot young people to research some of the cultural issues in their politically divided country.
- Many examples of participatory action research in Africa facilitated by Non Governmental Organizations (NGOs) where young people have substantial input into the design of the studies (e.g. *Phila Impilo!* (*www.icpcn.org.uk/core/ core_picker/download.asp?documenttable=libraryfiles&id=49*) [accessed 04/04/09]; Participatory Action Research in the Majority World (Nieuwenhuys, 2001); World Vision (www.worldvision.org.uk [accessed 17/02/09]); Save the Children (www. savethechildren.org.uk [accessed 17/02/09]); UNICEF South Africa (*www.unicef. org/infobycountry/southafrica.html* [accessed 17/02/09]).

Research example: are Harry Potter books too dangerous?

Here is a research summary, prepared by a Hungarian boy, about his investigation into whether Harry Potter books are too dangerous for primary school children (in Hungary primary schools are for children aged 8–14). I have not corrected any of the syntax because it is a reminder to us that English is not his first language.

Dear Audience!

My name is Norbert Gergály and I'm a fifth grade student in Primary and First Grade Art School of Zalabér. My topic is the Examination of Harry Potter books dangerousity in the circle of my schoolmates. I have chosen this topic, because I love Rowling's books. I'm interested in how did these religious and moral arguments develop. My aim is to examine if these books are really as dangerous as some people said.

My questions and hypotheisis wre the following:

- Have my schoolmates and teachers read the Harry Potter books?
- I thought they have.
- If somebody chooses an ideal from the books, does he choose a positive character?
- Before my examination I had thought that every boy does that.
- Why did this huge argument develope about the book.
- I thought because you can love or hate these books, but you can't be indifferent.
- Do my teachers think that the books are dangerous?
- I hoped they don't. I supposed that my teachers don't think that the books are occultists or dangerous.
- Do the children know that the books are just the creation of the imagination?

– I hoped that everyone knows it.

After I had read articles on the Internet, I started to write my essay. I have written the short stories of the five books, and I've introduced the main good and bad characters. Then I have made a questionary. I asked my teachers and schoolmates from the 4th to the 8th class. After they had answered my questions, I analysed their questionaries and compared them wit my hypotheisis.

I have found the following:

- Almost everybody heard about the Harry Potter books
- Just a few teachers and students have read them
- Most of my schoolmates have choosen positive characters to ideal, but for my big surprise some of them have chosen negative characters to like.
- Almost every child knows that the story is the creation of the fantasy, imagination.
- I was right, when I thougt that our teachers don't think that the book occult, but a few of them think it is dangerous. Our teachers would like us to read other books too, and one of them thinks that the film is garish.

After I have analyzed I think in the future too that the Harry Potter books aren't dangerous. I don't call in question the parents' responsibility. They must regard their children's range of interests. If they do that, they can prevent easily that children turn to occultism. They would rather have regard to help their children to see the positive values in the books.

Thank you for your attention.

Reflections on the research

Activity
What is Norbert trying to find out in his research? Consider that both adults and children have read – and watched – the Harry Potter books and it is a fair assumption to conclude that they are likely to respond differently to Harry Potter. There is more than children's enjoyment at stake here. What do you think are the issues from children's perspectives?

So far in this chapter we have examined why children and young people should undertake their own research and looked at some examples of this. The next part of the chapter moves on to where children's research is positioned in the bigger picture. How do adults receive research by children and can it influence policy making?

Can research by children and young people inform policy?

While we may undertake research for different purposes, what is common in all our research is that it generates data. The data generated can be used in different ways, e.g. to raise awareness, increase our knowledge and understanding and provide evidence to support hypotheses. Sometimes data might relate to matters of political governance, environmental significance or jurisprudence and can influence the formation of policy. Research on global warming, for instance, has influenced policies on carbon emissions. Research by children can and should inform policy since it generates new knowledge from children's perspectives that adults might not be able to access in the same way. However, influence brings responsibility. There is a responsibility to undertake reliable and valid research. Children, like adults, must expect their findings to be critically scrutinized. This is why it is so important to give children quality research training and help them develop valid research methods that will stand up to independent scrutiny. The scale and size of children's research is clearly important for any potential influence on policy. It may be that a small study can raise some awareness but a larger study would be needed to provide convincing evidence.

A concern I have is that we do not raise unrealistic expectations in children that their research is going to change the world. There have been some high profile examples of children's research influencing change – e.g. Shannon Davidson's research about what it is like for children living with a thyroid disorder (see Davidson, 2008 at http://childrens-research-centre.open.ac.uk [accessed 24/01/09]) influenced policy and practice at Great Ormond Street hospital – but not every piece of child-led research is going to have this kind of impact. Managing child researchers' outcome expectations is one of the responsibilities of adults who support them. Nonetheless, the targeted dissemination of valid research by children can raise awareness about issues and, in best circumstances, influence change. The example that follows illustrates some research by 11-year-olds about their literacy experiences. You can decide for yourselves how this might be used (or not used) to inform educational policy.

Research example: children researching literacy opportunities

Two groups of 11-year-old children, in socio-economically contrasting schools, carried out their own research on children's views about literacy opportunities (see Harry Rhodes, Liam Mark and Tom Perry (2007) http://childrens-research-centre. open.ac.uk [accessed 24/01/09]). The absence of power relations in the generation of child–child data avoided one of the common problems in adult–child data where children say what they think adults wants to hear in an attempt to 'please'. This freedom of expression was apparent in some children volunteering that their parents were too interfering and controlling about their homework and some were prepared to admit to books being pointless – views which might not have been offered as freely to an adult researcher, particularly a teacher researcher.

The child researchers identified confidence as a significant factor in educational achievement and explored levels of confidence children felt in their literacy skills (n = 80). Findings in the socio-economic area of advantage showed 100 per cent of girls and 88 per cent of boys rated their reading ability highly. Confidence in their speaking skills was also strong, with 80 per cent of them 'not minding explaining their thoughts in class'. The child researchers noticed that those aspects of reading and writing that were 'public' posed greater challenges for children's confidence. Reading out aloud was one of those challenges. More than half the respondents preferred not to read out aloud. Further findings also pointed to children being much less confident in writing than reading. These high levels of reading confidence and self-esteem were arrived at by ample opportunities to practise in private. However, children from an area of socio-economic disadvantage found few, if any, opportunities to practise their 'private' literacy confidence. Before they could face reading aloud, they needed lots of 'private practice' e.g. reading by themselves or reading in safe, non-threatening environments such as reading to younger siblings. Children talked about building up what they termed their 'private confidence' by reading on their own, sometimes rehearsing pronunciation and expression in whispers. As they grew in 'private confidence' they became less afraid of being called upon to read in class or to talk about what they had read in class. It was the facilitation of these opportunities in the home (quiet reading environments, encouragement to read as a leisure activity, plenty of books readily available) – and the *absence* of it for children living in an area of socio-economic disadvantage – which proved to be the biggest differentiator.

Writing was seen as the most public of all the literacy activities they engaged in. There are fewer opportunities to practise 'private' writing at home. Children viewed school writing as a painful process of endless drafts scrutinized by adults and publicly displayed around classroom walls. Private confidence developed through writing practice and resulted in a positive feeling towards that skill. Before children could develop confidence in their writing, they wanted opportunities to practise writing in situations where their efforts were not going to be public such as private journal writing time.

Reflections on the research

Activity

Think about how a reduction of power issues resulted in some data being generated that might not have been offered to adults. Can you find any specific examples of this in the extract?

Pause for thought

If adults had undertaken similar research they may not have accessed the issues and strength of feeling about building *private* literacy confidence, nor realized the extent of disadvantage from lack of *opportunity* to practise literacy skills experienced by children living in poverty. Listening to children's research voice is an important aspect of school transformation initiatives. It is worth reflecting for a moment on the extent to which the children's findings contradict many current classroom practices and the direction of educational reform. What is your view about whether this kind of research should inform policy discussion?

Research example: how safety-conscious are today's youth?

This research study was carried out by Carl Jones, a 17-year-old youth in 2005. You can read his full research report on the Children's Research Centre website at http://childrens-research-centre.open.ac.uk [accessed 24/01/09]. Carl distributed a questionnaire to 80 peers and held several focus group interviews. His study explored what factors young people identified as dangers and what precautions, if any, they took to try and stay safe. He identified themes of peer pressure, bullying, gang intimidation, mugging/theft, drugs and drink spiking. Here is an extract from his report.

> Peer pressure included being persuaded to have sex at an early age, to drink, to smoke or to take drugs. They commented that peer pressure is ultimately doing something of your own accord, unlike bullying when you may be physically forced to do something. However they said that people often cave-in to peer pressure because they do not want to 'look the odd one out' and they 'feel they'll be left out' if they do not conform. They all seemed to believe that peer pressure was potentially very dangerous and that it did exist in their community. (p. 3)

A surprising finding in Carl's study was that despite all the perceived dangers, young people were selective in the steps they took to safeguard themselves. For example most of the young people volunteered that they kept mobile phones and valuables hidden to protect against mugging but over 86 per cent said they never carry a personal safety alarm and Carl's research found only one individual who always carried one.

Possibly such an action is not seen as being 'socially acceptable'. The focus group remarked that personal safety alarms are too big to carry around. They feared that friends 'take the mick' if they know you have such a device. The group believed that it is best to try to defend yourself or run away as the general public rarely respond to alarms if they are set off. They felt this was because 'everyone feels someone else will help', known in Psychology as Genovese Syndrome. Another suggested reason was that it is not easy to recognise a personal safety alarm from a car alarm or other similar device, hence people do not realise there is a fellow human in danger. . . . The interviewees believed that more people might carry a personal safety alarm if they were given out, perhaps in schools, and that the benefits of carrying one were explained by an authority figure. Even still, they felt boys would rather 'stick up for themselves' than set off an alarm. (p. 8)

Reflections on the research

Activity

Consider this quote from Carl's study (p. 9) about young people's choice of dress.

They believed the clothes you wear send out a message and from this you know 'what to expect from people and what kind of people they are', though they felt people should not be judged by their clothes as everyone should have the free right to express themselves. People who follow a particular stereotype with their dress, for example goths and chavs, realise it puts them in danger but asserted that they still do not deserve to be attacked. They extended this to cover women who wear short skirts to go out. They stressed that they do not deserve to be attacked or raped and felt they are not at fault at all if this happens. They also commented that the risks are reduced by being with a group of people all dressed the same.

The group spoke strongly about not being allowed to wear hoods in shopping centres because of associations with stealing and vandalism, despite religious headgear being openly accepted. Clearly some young people feel under attack because of their clothes and are responding by attacking another group. If you are being accused of being a potential criminal because of your clothes, it breeds resentment. How we choose to dress is clearly an important part of who we are and how we feel about ourselves, and care has to be taken when we make assumptions based on peoples' clothes.

Do you think the data would have been different if it had been collected by an adult?

How important do you think this kind of data is for our understanding of today's youth? Can and should it inform policy?

Interview with Dr Darren Sharpe about young researchers

Dr Darren Sharpe is Youth Researcher Network Co-ordinator, National Youth Organisation, UK.

Mary: Can you tell me a little about the Young Researcher Network?

Darren: The Young Researcher Network is a project part of The National Youth Agency and since September 2007 we have supported fifteen groups of young people in doing youth-led research projects on matters that affects their lives. The network values, supports, and encourages research led by young people, provides on-line resources and seeks out opportunities for young people to speak directly with decision makers.

Mary: In your view what are the main barriers to young people carrying out their own research?

Darren: The barriers to young people carrying out research are numerous. For me the big three are; the perception of research as an exclusively adult activity, the apathy of young people taking-up new research projects caused by the bureaucratic black hole and the lack of organizational support for young people interested in doing research. When young people cannot see where or how their research has contributed to change apathy easily creeps-in and will deter young people from taking on new research projects. When academics, senior mangers and policy makers pull the rug from beneath the young researchers' feet by overly scrutinizing research feelings of success quickly turn into failure. This often happens when the same lens is used to measure and ultimately judge young researchers work in the same light as professional researchers. Finally, when organizations and support workers underestimate the volume of work involved in supporting groups of young researchers and respond inaptly it negatively impacts on the young researcher and the research project.

Mary: You spend a lot of your time supporting young people with their research, what are the highs and lows of this role?

Darren: One of the biggest joys in supporting young people in doing research is witnessing the transformation that often occurs as they absorb new information and take on research practices that they make their own.

Young people telling their own unscripted stories – often without too much adult interference – will yield surprises. It's also exciting watching how children and young people locate their own lives or set of circumstances in the complex web of social relationships and institutions and see the world anew. This then tells me that they will take something away from the research far behind the rigours of doing the research itself. These instances are always fleeting but bring a smile to my face whenever they occur.

It is also a very good sign when children and young people feel confident and supported to take ownership of the project (or aspects of it). But research by its very nature is not tangible and straight forward; consequently, ownership is not easily achieved. It takes a leap in imagination and a sophisticated style of project management to which only time and experience can bring.

The low points of supporting young researchers is when the methodology is predetermined even before the research question is known and reinforced through aggressive gate keeping by adult support workers. There is an evangelical thread that runs through many children and youth work services that can close down methodological discussions. This is sometimes translated into very specific ways of working which hamper the development and implementation of young people's research. I feel it denies young people the chance of becoming aware of research in its broadest and richest sense. It is not an exclusive club but social researchers belong to a fraternity of the inquisitive, the questioning and the socially consciousness.

Where to next?

In predicting where child-led research is heading in the future it is helpful to turn to the past. Feminist, race and disability research are all predicated on 'insider perspective' (Kellett, 2005a) and their historical trails illustrate the trajectory that child-led research – the newest 'insider perspective' research approach – is likely to take. Over time, I think repositories dedicated to children's research will be established, some of these may take on traditional adult forms such as e-journals but more of them are likely to adopt child-friendly resource banks such as websites (e.g. www.nya/youngresearchernetwork.org. uk and http://childrens-research-centre.open.ac.uk [accessed 24/01/09]), rights-based homes (e.g. www.crae.org and www.crin.org [accessed 02/02/09]), children's charities such as www.unicef.org.uk [accessed 17/02/09] and others, chat rooms in virtual environments and drama-driven road shows. More politically-weighted children's research may be housed within youth decision-making forums. Unless adult–child power relational issues can be skilfully negotiated in school contexts the hub of children's research is likely to be located away from school environments. This would be unfortunate because school contexts offer a common space where adult and child perspectives are constantly thrown together and the opportunities for mutual enlightenment are endless. Children's school experiences constitute a very large part of their childhood and it is important that children continue to research educational issues from their perspectives. Their experiences outside school are also formative and child-led research here will bring adults and children closer to a shared understanding of contemporary childhoods.

Key points

- Research by children must be robust and valid and able to stand up to independent scrutiny if it is to influence policy.
- We need to be careful not to raise unrealistic expectations in children about the potential influence their research might have.
- Some research by children can, and has, influenced change.
- As the incidence of children's research grows appropriate dissemination outlets need to be found.

Summary

This chapter has:
- Considered the concept of children and young people as researchers in their own right.
- Discussed the benefits of children's research in society at large.
- Constructed a rationale for the importance of children undertaking their own research.
- Explored critical issues, such as how young children can start doing research.
- Provided examples of children's original research studies.
- Given consideration to the role that research by children can play in informing policy and practice.

Suggested further reading

Kellett, M. (2005) *How to Develop Children as Researchers: A Step by Step Guide to Teaching Research Process*, London: Paul Chapman.

This book gives step-by-step support for anyone wanting to train and support children as researchers in their own right.

Warming, H. (2006) '"How can you know? You're not a foster child": dilemmas and possibilities of giving voice to children in foster care', *Children Youth and Environments*, 16, 2, 28–50.

This article describes an action research project in Denmark called 'Children's Parliament' and discusses how children's lived experiences of foster care can be voiced to inform policy and practice.

http://childrens-research-centre.open.ac.uk [accessed 24/01/09]

This website features over 100 original research studies by children and young people. You can search on age or year submitted.

www.nya.org.uk/yrn [accessed 24/01/09]

This is the website of the Young Researcher Network which features research by young people, news items and a blog.

Part 3
Policy and Practice Issues

Implications for Policy and Practice and Impact on Children's Lives

7

Chapter Outline

Introduction and key questions

I hope it has become clear in the preceding chapters that research involving children has a major part to play in the shaping of contemporary society. If the purpose of research is to increase knowledge and understanding in order to benefit society then the impact of child research should be visible in policy and practice that benefit children. This final chapter focuses on the implications for policy and practice of research involving children. It draws on some specific examples of impact but also discusses where research is *not* having impact and why this might be. I concentrate mainly on the UK but make reference to situations in other countries to help situate the main drivers connecting research and policy in a global context.

- Do politics inhibit the impact of research involving children?
- What are the implications of child research for childhoods?
- How is research involving children informing policy globally?
- Can research undertaken by children and young people influence policy and practice?

Do politics inhibit the impact of research involving children?

There have been some landmark policies regarding children and young people in recent years – e.g. *Every Child Matters* (2003); *Children Act* (2004); *Youth Matters* (2005); *Youth Matters: Next Steps* (2006); and the *Children's Plan* (2008). Such policies are constructed from a combination of research evidence, wide consultation data and think tank stimuli. It is difficult to separate politics from policy and the more cynical might argue that policy is driven as much by vote winning initiatives and media responses as by grass roots research. High profile child deaths have been very influential in shaping child care policy. The tragic death of Victoria Climbie in 2000 and the systemic failures it exposed brought about a radical shake-up of children's services. It gave impetus to an integrated approach and an emphasis on multi-agency working, embedded in the Every Child Matters agenda.

Youth Matters (2005) and its sequel *Youth Matters: Next Steps* (2006) professed to be an extension of this thinking to older children but the length of time to get from *Every Child Matters* to *Youth Matters* suggests that this was not a particular priority for the Government. Coincidentally, the publication of the policy followed an avalanche of negative media coverage on yobbish youth behaviour and it is interesting to note that anti-social behaviour makes an appearance very early in the document – by point 7, of 41 – in the *Youth Matters* Executive Summary: 'A minority of young people can get involved in behaviour that is a serious problem for the wider community, including anti-social behaviour and crime. The Government is clear that when this happens we need to respond firmly.'

The *Children's Plan* (2008) is probably the least reactive of the policy documents mentioned above and the most informed by research. It followed the 2007 UNICEF report on children's wellbeing which placed British children at the bottom of the 'happiness' rankings. The stinging influence of this research is evident from the very first sentence of the Secretary of State's Foreword, 'Our aim is to make this the best place in the world for our children and young people to grow up'.

The *Children's Plan* (2008, 3) sets out a 10-year strategy aimed at improving the lives of children.

> Based on our consultation, five principles underpin the Children's Plan:
>
> - government does not bring up children – parents do – so;
> - government needs to do more to back parents and families;
> - all children have the potential to succeed and should go as far as their talents can take them;
> - children and young people need to enjoy their childhood as well as grow up prepared for adult life;
> - services need to be shaped by and responsive to children, young people and families, not designed around professional boundaries; and
> - it is always better to prevent failure than tackle a crisis later.

Sometimes the contribution of research to policy is ambivalent especially when a research inquiry is controlled by those holding the policy reins. For example, consider this quote from the *Children's Plan* (2008, 10) relating to primary children's education.

> We have announced a root and branch review of the primary curriculum, led by Sir Jim Rose, to ensure there is:
>
> - more time for the basics so children achieve a good grounding in reading, writing and mathematics;
> - greater flexibility for other subjects;
> - time for primary school children to learn a modern foreign language; and
> - a smoother transition from play-based learning in the early years into primary school, particularly to help summer-born children who can be at a disadvantage when they enter primary school.

It suggests that the Government, in commissioning a 'root and branch review of the primary curriculum', is making a statement about valuing the knowledge and understanding that research will bring but at the same time is predetermining what it wants the research to find out (as indicated in the four cited bullet points). It cannot be a root and branch review if a lack of independence pre-determines which roots and branches may or may not be examined. When the Secretary of State commissioned the primary review he told Sir Jim Rose, 'Your review is focused on the curriculum and is not considering changes to the current assessment and testing regime' (BBC News 20/10/08, http:// news.bbc.co.uk/1/hi/education/7680895.stm [accessed 21/11/08]). Indeed, when it was published, one of the main criticisms of the Interim Rose Report (8 December 2008) was that it failed to look at a number of critical factors that were affecting the quality of children's primary school experiences – notably testing and assessment.

> On the one hand, it recommends six themed 'areas of learning', which – and Jim Rose is keen to emphasis this – will still include all the traditional subject areas. At the same time, the review says there should be greater emphasis on literacy, numeracy and ICT (information and communication technology), space should be made for modern foreign languages and schools should find more time to teach about personal skills and sex and relationships education. This is not 'de-cluttering' the curriculum. They have simply moved everything around, renamed a few things, and thrown a few more things on top.
>
> The second problem with the review is that it fails to take the testing regime into account. The greatest block to primary schools – and their capacity to develop – is not the curriculum but the way they are tested and held to account by Government. Key Stage tests have proven clumsy, narrow and of no significant purpose for the children themselves. Primary schools already have a tremendous capacity and appetite for curriculum development; it is the tests, not the content of the curriculum that is holding most back. (*The Telegraph* 8/12/08 www.telegraph.co. uk/education/3684693 [accessed 21/11/08])

It is astonishing that a review putatively examining an over-crowded and allegedly ineffective primary curriculum could have no scope to look at one of the largest consumers of curricular time – assessment. Outside of his review, Sir Jim Rose spoke openly about time spent on over-preparing for tests and of assessment as the 'elephant in the room' but he was unable to include testing and assessment in his review. As long as these kinds of constraints are imposed by those commissioning and funding research (in this case the UK government) such research can only make a limited – and some would argue 'flawed' – contribution to policy making. Moreover, until research about children routinely *involves* children there will continue to be an important dimension missing from the knowledge generated on which policy decisions are based.

Pause for thought

In the construction of the Interim Rose Report (2008), a wide range of evidence was drawn upon

> the extensive databases of the QCA, Ofsted, the National College for School Leadership (NCSL), the Training and Development Agency for Schools (TDA), the National Strategies and the DCSF. Views have been sought from a wide range of stakeholders, including teacher unions, professional bodies, specially convened groups of head teachers and teachers, inspectors and advisers, teacher trainers, researchers and subject specialists. Much helpful information has also stemmed from unsolicited contributions from individuals and groups, such as parents and carers. (p. 9)

What important group of individuals is missing from the list? Yes, you are right, there are no children!

Governments in some countries are more proactive at eliciting the views of children about their citizenship and their rights such as the series of focus groups set up in New Zealand schools to discover children's views on their understanding of citizenship issues. The children reported on their rights and responsibilities in the everyday contexts of home, school and community (see Taylor et al., 2008).

Research example: the Rose and Alexander reports

In determining the effect of independent research versus government-controlled research it is useful to compare the findings of the *Rose Report* commissioned by Government with *The Cambridge Primary Review Special Report on the Curriculum* (February 2009 – known as the Alexander Report) commissioned by Cambridge University and funded by the Esmee Fairbairn Foundation. Here is an extract from the Alexander Report:

> The most conspicuous casualties are the arts, the humanities and those kinds of learning in all subjects which require time for talking, problem-solving and the extended exploration of ideas; memorisation and recall have come to be valued over understanding and enquiry, and transmission of information over the pursuit of knowledge in its fuller sense.

. . .

A curriculum should reflect and enact educational aims and values, but during the past two decades national aims and curriculum have been separately determined, making the aims cosmetic and the true purposes of primary education opaque. In a complex and changing world there is an urgent need for proper debate about what primary education is for. This debate was pre-empted when the national curriculum was introduced in 1988–9, and again when it was reviewed in 1997–8. It must not happen in 2009.

. . .

Fuelling these problems has been a policy-led belief that curriculum breadth is incompatible with the pursuit of standards in 'the basics' and that if anything gives way it must be breadth. Evidence going back many decades, including reports from HMI and Ofsted, consistently shows this belief to be unfounded. Standards and breadth are interdependent, and high-performing schools achieve both.

. . .

Micro-management by DCSF, the national agencies and national strategies is widely perceived to be excessive and to have contributed to some of the problems above. Curriculum debate, and thus curriculum practice, is weakened by a muddled and reductive discourse about subjects, knowledge and skills. Discussion of the place of subjects is needlessly polarised; knowledge is grossly parodied as grubbing for obsolete facts; and the undeniably important notion of skill is inflated to cover aspects of learning for which it is not appropriate. There is an urgent need for key curriculum terms to be clarified and for the level of curriculum discussion and conceptualisation to be raised. Re-naming components of the curriculum 'skills', 'themes' or 'areas of learning' does not of itself address the fundamental question of what primary education is about; nor does it necessarily make the curriculum more manageable in practice. (Cambridge Primary Review Briefing paper, p. 1–2 www.primaryreview.org.uk [accessed 21/11/08])

Reflections on the research

Activity

From this extract of the Alexander Report can you identify examples which indicate that this is an independent research inquiry? Think about how this kind of research could influence children's education policy? What might get in the way? – e.g. are any aspects in the extract critical of a government department or government policy? Are there major funding implications for some of the recommendations?

You might like to read the full text of both the Rose Report and the Alexander Report to do a more extensive comparison. The references for these are provided in the Suggested further reading at the end of the chapter.

It is in the nature of politics that governments always need to put a positive spin on their policies and are not seen to be making mistakes. This can get in the way of best practice if the defence of ailing policies takes precedence over addressing critical fallout. At a simplistic level, this is what has happened with the over-testing of children in schools. Measuring standards became a government mantra, schools were pitted against each other in competitive league tables and the result was a curriculum driven by testing. Teaching to tests breeds a diet of shallow, rote learning which squeezes out depth, breadth and the critical and exploratory aspects of learning. The price of this has been a generation of children ill-served by an inferior education system. Academic research (e.g. Sturman, 2003; Meadows et al., 2008) had been pointing to this for years but was failing to influence change because the government of the day did not want to listen to findings which undermined one of its flagship policies. Research can only have an impact if an audience is willing to listen and act. Otherwise change happens very slowly and too late for some children. The debate about taking politics out of education is beyond the scope of this book but taking politics out of research is not, and warrants serious consideration.

The influence of politics can be neutralized to some extent when research is undertaken at an international level. One such example is a longitudinal, international study of reading achievement in 40 countries, the PIRLS (Progress in International Reading Literacy Study) reports. Data were collected in 2001 and reported in 2003 and then further data were collected in 2006 and reported in 2007. A third set of data is planned to be collected in 2011. The children involved in the study were aged 9–10 years. The first PIRLS report (see Sainsbury et al., 2004) placed England third out of 35 participating countries in reading achievement from data collected in 2001. The second PIRLS report (see Mullis et al., 2007) placed England nineteenth out of 40 participating countries from data collected in 2006. In 5 years, despite all the money invested in primary literacy, back to basics and other government initiatives reading standards in England would appear to have plummeted.

Activity

Research evidence indicated falling reading standards in England (Mullis et al., 2007) and rising child poverty in real terms (Christensen and Prout, 2005). Nevertheless, the Secretary of State wrote in the Foreword to *The Children's Plan*:

We heard that while there are more opportunities for young people today than ever before, parents want more support in managing the new pressures they face such as balancing work and family life, dealing with the internet and the modern commercial world, and letting their children play and learn whilst staying safe. We heard that while children are doing better than ever in school, we need to do more to ensure that every child gets a world class education. We heard that while fewer children now live in poverty, too many children's education is still being held back by poverty and disadvantage. (Children's Plan, 2008, Executive Summary, p. 1)

Make a note of any words you can identify as being 'spin'. Think about the relationship between spin and research. Does the presence of spin enhance or weaken the efficacy of the research?

Pause for thought

Not all research has beneficial outcomes for children. For example the IQ tests developed by Stanford-Binet in 1910 were based on extensive research, just as the Standardised Assessment Tasks (SATS) of the 1990s claimed to be, but either would be hard-pressed to demonstrate any positive benefits for children. Research that led to the forced removal of Aboriginal children from their indigenous families in the early twentieth century and placement with white Australian families and/or institutions allegedly to improve their life chances was atrociously harmful despite the system being labelled 'child welfare'. It was a system of domination deliberately designed to eliminate their parents' culture and society (see Van Krieken, 1992).

Key points

- Politics can sometimes impede the impact research has on policy. This can happen when research findings conflict with government agendas or when the parameters of the research are constrained by government commissioning bodies.
- Care needs to be taken to separate out political spin from research evidence.
- Not all research has beneficial outcomes for children.

What are the implications of child research for childhoods?

This section examines the implications of child research on policy issues related to the quality of childhoods: the impact research involving children is having on children's worlds. The public and private spaces children inhabit can be divided into two main environments of school and home. We have already considered some implications of research for children's school experiences. In this section I explore some implications of research on the private spaces they inhabit.

Research example: *The Good Childhood Inquiry*

This was an independent inquiry into contemporary UK childhood commissioned by The Children's Society charity. You can access the full research report in Layard, R. and Dunn, J. (2009) *A Good Childhood: Searching for values in a competitive age*, London: Penguin. The research had six themes: friends, family, learning, lifestyle, health and values. Survey and focus group evidence was contributed by over 30,000 people including more than 20,000 children. The research focused around the following questions:

- What are the conditions for a good childhood?
- What obstacles exist to those conditions today?
- What changes could be made which on the basis of evidence would be likely to improve things? These may be changes in the behaviour of parents, teachers, government, voluntary sector or faith organizations, or in society at large.

Evidence was provided in the following way:

- 2,006 people contributed to two early NOP polls, one poll of adults and one of children, which helped identify the main issues for the inquiry to focus on.
- 3,579 people – almost all adults – took part in a series of polls run by GfK NOP Reflections on childhood based on the themes of the inquiry.
- Around 8,000 children took part in research commissioned by The Children's Society.
- 1,626 adults and professionals responded to our call for evidence.
- 742 children responded to our call for evidence.
- 13,389 responses were received from children taking part in two series of polls, one run by BBC Newsround and one on The Children's Society's My Life website.
- 5,050 children sent in postcards with evidence.
- Around 300 children were involved in 50 focus groups with hard-to-reach children.

(www.childrenssociety.org.uk [accessed 25/03/09])

From all the evidence collected the Inquiry panel made the following recommendations, directly to the government (they also made recommendations to other bodies too) aimed at helping them to achieve quality childhood experiences for all children:

- Introduce non religious, free civil birth ceremonies.
- Offer high quality parenting classes, psychological support and adolescent mental health services throughout the country.
- Train at least 1,000 more highly qualified psychological therapists over the next five years.
- Automatically assess the mental health of children entering local authority care or custody.
- Raise the pay and status of all people who work with children including teachers and child care workers.
- Give a salary supplement to teachers taking jobs in deprived areas.
- Replace all SATS tests with an annual assessment designed mainly to guide a child's learning.
- Stop publishing data on individual schools from which league tables are constructed by the media.
- Start a major campaign to persuade employers to offer apprenticeships.
- Build a high quality youth centre for every 5,000 young people.
- Ban all building on sports fields and open spaces where children play.
- Ban firms from advertising to British children under 12.
- Ban adverts for alcohol or unhealthy food on television before 9 pm.
- Reduce the proportion of children in relative poverty from 22% to under 10% by 2015.

(www.childrenssociety.org.uk [accessed 25/03/09])

Reflections on the research

Activity

At the time of writing this, the *Good Childhood Inquiry* is a recent publication. Its findings were launched only a few months ago. It is too early to evaluate what influence it will have on policy and practice and how this might impact on the quality of childhoods but it is widely expected that this will be a landmark research study. Do you agree with the recommendations? Which (if any) of its recommendations do you think a government might adopt? Consider whether any of the recommendations align with current government policy – if so do you think they might be more likely to be adopted than those that do not (such as the replacement of SATS). Also consider how much the recommendations might cost a government e.g. raising the pay and status of all people who work with children would be very expensive compared to the cost of starting a campaign to persuade employers to offer apprenticeships. Do you think some of its recommendations will find their way into practice even without government legislation? For example, local councils control planning permission so this might enable a ban on building on sports fields to be realized.

Pause for thought

The findings of the *Good Childhood Inquiry* were launched in a blaze of media publicity at Central Hall, Westminster on 4th February 2009. The Children's Society ran a high profile dissemination campaign which found its way to all the major newspapers and news channels. Consider the extent to which influential research leverage is determined by the mode of dissemination?

How is research involving children informing policy and practice at a global level?

It took 10 years of research and consultation before the UNCRC was finally launched in 1989. However, this edict has had unparalleled impact on children's lives globally. It is an international human rights treaty that grants all children and young people a comprehensive set of rights. The convention sets out 41 articles which include children's right to:

- Special protection measures and assistance.
- Access to services such as education and health care.
- Develop their personalities, abilities and talents to the fullest potential.
- Grow up in an environment of happiness, love and understanding.
- Be informed about and participate in achieving their rights in an accessible and active manner.

Articles 42–54 relate to the responsibility of participating states to implement the 41 children's rights articles.

What has made the difference between the UNCRC being a document that sits gathering dust on government shelves around the world and one that creates impact has been the setting up of the UNCRC Committee. This is a United Nations treaty monitoring body which assesses how well states are implementing the convention, reports on progress and makes recommendations. States which signed up to the convention (that is, all States except USA and Somalia) have to report to the Committee on their implementation progress. The committee comprises 18 independent children's rights experts who are elected in their personal capacity to 4-year terms. The committee meets three times a year in Geneva, Switzerland.

Policy to practice example: UN Committee on the Rights of the Child

Here is an example from the UK's Consolidated Third and Fourth Periodic Report to the UN Committee on the Rights of the Child (DCSF, 2007). The UK Government first reported back to the UN Committee in 1994 and then again in 1999. Its third and fourth submissions were merged into one document which was submitted in 2007. Participating governments have to respond directly to any issues raised by the UN Committee from their previous Periodic Report (i.e. in this case from the UK's Second Periodic Report, 1999). This is an issue that was picked up by the UN Committee from that 1999 report.

> The Committee encourages the State party [UK] to expedite the adoption and implementation of a comprehensive plan of action for the implementation of the Convention in all parts of the State party, taking into account The Way Forward for Care and paying special attention to children belonging to the most vulnerable groups (e.g. children from poor households, children from minority groups, disabled children, homeless children, children in care, children between 16 and 18, Irish and Roma travellers' children and asylum-seekers) through an open, consultative and participatory process' (p. 19 of The Consolidated 3rd and 4th Periodic Report to the UN Committee on the Rights of the Child, DCSF, 2007)

The UK Government responded with four plans of action (one for each of the nation states). They encapsulate the essence of what is now commonly known as *Every Child Matters*. This is the plan of action for England (DCSF, 2007, 19–20).

> **1.24** *Every Child Matters* is a set of reforms – supported by the Children Act 2004 designed to enable families, local communities and services to work together to improve the lives of all 0 to 19 year olds and narrow the gap between those who do well and those who do not. *Every Child Matters* measures progress in improving the lives of children and young people in five broad areas (known as outcomes, which are enshrined in law through the Children Act 2004): health; safety; achievement & enjoyment; making a positive contribution; and achieving economic well-being.

> **1.25** *Every Child Matters* integrates universal targeted and specialist services for children and young people from 0–19, bringing services together around the needs of children. It enables children's services to work across professional boundaries, using common processes and terms of reference. *Every Child Matters* has established children's trusts as commissioners of services for children, young people and families, driven forward by Directors of Children's Services in each local authority. Local areas carry out joint analysis of the needs of their local population and prioritise and plan their services, in conjunction with service users, through a Children and Young People's Plan. The process is a continuous cycle of consultation, evaluation, planning and commissioning of services for children.

1.26 *Every Child Matters* has been widely supported across central and local government, the voluntary and community sector and amongst front-line staff. It has been followed up by a series of policy documents looking at particular areas of policy in more detail – i.e. *Youth Matters; A Ten Year Childcare Strategy; Every Parent Matters.* Special attention has also been paid to vulnerable groups through *Care Matters; the Special Educational Needs (SEN) strategy* and the new strategy for disabled children. As a result, the lives of children and young people are being increasingly improved. For example:

- Over 600,000 children have been lifted out of relative poverty since 1998–99, and there has been a faster fall in child poverty in the UK than in any other EU country over the same period.
- The gap has narrowed in the achievement of minority ethnic pupils, with the proportion of both Black Caribbean and Bangladeshi pupils achieving 5 or more A* to C grades at GCSE, or their equivalent, in 2006 up 10 percentage points since 2003, compared to a national increase of 6 percentage points for all pupils.
- Participation among 16 year olds has increased to its highest ever level, with 89% in some form of learning in 2005–06.
- Over 1,250 children's centres and over 4,000 extended schools have been created, ahead of the trajectory that will deliver 3,500 children's centres, and on track for all schools to be extended schools, by 2010.
- The Youth Opportunity and Youth Capital Funds have invested £115 million over 2006–08 to provide young people with more choice and influence over facilities in their area.
- Over £130 million has been invested since 2002 in Creative Partnerships, involving over 500,000 children in creativity and arts projects.

Activity

List any evidence you can find in the extract to show that the *Every Child Matters* plan of action is having a beneficial impact on vulnerable groups of children and young people? Do you think the government has responded appropriately to the prompt from the UN Committee?

It is interesting to compare the UK response to the UNCRC Committee with other country responses. One such is Norway's fourth response to the Committee (2008). Part of their preparation for that response was to involve 1,274 children as participants in a research project to ascertain children's views about the UNCRC and its impact on their lives.

The survey showed that about half of the children and young people in the partici-pating municipalities knew of the UN Convention on the Rights of the Child.

A higher proportion knew that they had rights. Teaching and enforcement of children's rights at school and in their leisure time can without doubt be improved. The survey brought to light wide municipal variations. Hence an important conclusion is that there are no institutional safeguards to ensure that children and young people in Norway are made aware of the Convention, of their own rights and the significance to them of such rights.

Children and young people were quick to respond on the issue of deciding over their personal everyday life. One young person put it as follows: 'Just because we have a good life doesn't mean that we can demand everything we want. We also have obligations.' They were also preoccupied with combating bullying and discrimination in Norway, and children's situation in other parts of the world meant a lot to them. It will be important to build on this readiness to assume responsibility in the further planning of tuition in children's and young people's rights. (Sandaek and Einarsson, 2008, 61–62)

Pause for thought

The UN Committee prompt came from the UK Periodic Report of 1999. It was 4 years before the Every Child Matters green paper (2003) emerged and 8 years before an action plan was reported back to the UN Committee. What is your view about these time scales?

In the era of cyberspace and 24-hour news programmes, 'global' readily becomes 'local' and information is communicated quickly and extensively. This is especially true for NGOs who have sophisticated websites. In virtual environments, research has the potential to be very influential. Moreover, muted and marginalized voices can sometimes succeed in getting their voices heard in cyberspace where this would not have been possible in more conventional political space (Ong, 2006). An example is young people in China using the internet to protest their human rights (see Hartas, 2008).

To be influential child research does not have to be a large scale national or international project or a government commissioned review. Sometimes action research projects spring up around themes that have only just started to be debated in the public arena and can influence policy formation while it is still at an embryonic stage. An example is the current debate surrounding the part young people might play in school improvement processes through distributed leadership schemes where students are 'partners' in transformative activity.

Research example: student involvement in school transformation

This example illustrates a school community of practice where all school participants, whether they are staff or students, have the potential to bring about change through engagement in transformative processes. It is an action research project undertaken at a comprehensive school in the London Borough of Hackney (Bucknall, 2009). The project was run through the School Council which set up a sixth-form committee with four sub-committees of elected representatives for each of four areas of research: *safety and well being; school environment (including teaching and learning); lunch-time environment; and social and cultural practices.* A group of students in Year 8 (aged 13) were trained in research methods and then identified issues to investigate from within the four themed areas. They prepared proposals to the School Council on what they wanted to research and the School Council decided which proposals to 'commission'. Once they had completed their research projects the young researchers reported their findings and recommendations back to the School Council. The School Council then took responsibility for taking forward these outcomes to the Governing Body where action decisions were taken. This process enabled students to be actively involved in the process of change in a transformative way. Students reported that it made them feel valued and listened to (Bucknall, 2009).

> 'For them to take us seriously was kinda weird. They were listening to what we had to say and what the students said so that they could make changes 'cause of what we thought and not what they thought and I felt really included.' (Ogechi, Student Researcher)

> 'And we were telling them and not them telling us
> – we knew something they didn't know about.'
> ('How did that make you feel?')
> 'Powerful.' (Anna, Student Researcher)

> 'You're part of something important in school.' (Francesca, Student Researcher)

Pause for thought

There are two sides to any coin and the flip side of agency via school council representation is that this may come at the cost of individual voices being marginalized because they have to rely on others to articulate their concerns. So the picture is not all rosy or positive and it is worth bearing in mind that the new power relations created by school councils can lead to a lack of shared agendas and some negative impacts (Bucknall, 2009).

> **Key points**
>
> - Quality child research can inform policy about contemporary childhoods and this impact can be magnified by high profile dissemination.
> - Cyberspace provides an additional milieu where research can influence policy and can provide a voice for groups who are marginalized in physical space.
> - Small research projects can still exert influence and can stimulate debate around important childhood themes.

Can research undertaken by children and young people influence policy and practice?

Chapter 6 explored several examples of research by children and young people and the argument about efficacy is already made. In this section I look more particularly at the *impact* that child-led research might have on policy and practice. To do this I have chosen an example of research by some young asylum seekers.

According to the United Nations High Commission for Refugees (UNHCR, 2007, 30) 596,000 people applied for asylum worldwide during 2006. The UK received the fifth highest number of asylum seekers at 27,800. Nearly half of all refugees are children (Pandya, 2007) which translates into substantial numbers of children and young people, many of them unaccompanied, who are refugees or asylum seekers (RAS). Language and culture are frequent barriers to service provision. Asylum seekers were one of the vulnerable groups of children identified by the UN Committee (see earlier section in this chapter) as needing support. This UNCRC Policy to Practice example illustrated that it can take several years for policy action plans to address critical issues. An alternative approach is to engage in research initiatives which have an immediate and direct impact on practice. Outcomes may ultimately influence policy in the longer term but benefits for vulnerable children have a desirable immediacy.

Research example: the Routz Project

You can read the full research report in Raksha Pandya's (2007) 'Working with young refugees and asylum seekers through participatory action research in health promotion'. In M. Sallah and C. Howson (eds) *Working with Black young people,* Lyme Regis: Russell House Publishing.

> At a refugee and asylum seekers (RAS) forum it was anecdotally identified that some newly arrived young (16–24 year old) RAS from Iraq, Iran, Afghanistan and Albania were drinking large quantities of alcohol and smoking cannabis and that they did not know the difference in potency between a pint of beer and a pint of vodka or the effects of smoking cannabis and other harder drugs.
>
> . . .
>
> At the same time, the University of Central Lancashire was running the Department of Health's BME substance needs assessment project called the Community Engagement Programme [CEP]. The CEP was undertaking its third year investigating nationally the drug and alcohol related needs of marginalised groups. Through this scheme Turning Point Loughborough and Northwest Lancashire decided to carry out some research into this group of RAS to:
>
> - Explore the current and perceived alcohol and drug use issues amongst RAS.
> - Clarify the issues surrounding problem drinking/drug use amongst this group of individuals.
> - Identify current levels of understanding around substance misuse.
> - Identify potential gaps in service provision.
>
> Like any other BME community member, not born in the UK, RAS were likely to experience language barriers and differences in cultures when speaking with other people from a different background. Additionally further anecdotal evidence suggested that some RAS had not heard of what a substance misuse service was or what one did. Therefore it was clear that the research needed to be carried out by the RAS themselves. Turning Point approached existing Refugee Community Organisations (RCO) to locate RAS who may have wished to be involved in this research study. . . . Eventually Turning Point recruited two people to drive the actual work through the technique of Participatory Action Research (PAR). The RAS researchers were trained by University of Central Lancashire through six days of intensive training on drugs and alcohol research methods.
>
> Two research methods used by the researchers were focus groups and structured interviews. In total 46 participants took part.

It appeared from the research that RAS have a particular vulnerability to substance misuse. Furthermore accommodation for those seeking asylum can sometimes be shared with drug users and exposure to substances more generally seemed to happen both in transit and in the early stages of arrival. Many of the participants were aware of where to get drugs and had been offered substances. The vulnerability of young unaccompanied asylum seekers and refugees was compounded with increased isolation, insecurity and anxiety, as well as a lack of knowledge and understanding of substance misuse. (Pandya, 2007, 126–128)

The research had an immediate impact. Local commissioners, policy makers and strategists made positive adjustments to the way these young people were supported. Additional resources were accessed from the local drug and alcohol action team and more preventative measures were able to be introduced in culturally sensitive ways.

Reflections on the research

Activity 1

The research increased knowledge and understanding about the needs of young RAS in relation to substance misuse. Reflect on the difference involving young RAS themselves to collect peer-to-peer data, without language barriers, made to this research.

Activity 2

Take a few moments to imagine what it must be like for an unaccompanied young asylum seeker, arriving in Britain with no English, no family, no possessions and a multitude of traumatic memories to deal with. How easy would it be for such a person to fall prey to substance misuse? How do you think the Routz project is raising awareness? How could this be developed further?

This section began by posing a question about whether research undertaken by young people can influence policy and practice. The examples cited here, and in the previous chapter, suggest that there is clear potential for this to happen and that young people's research can contribute valuable knowledge and insights. However, issues which prevent this being as positive an experience as it might include limited funding to support young people's research and the difficulties of getting their research voices heard by policy makers. This contrasts with experiences in some other countries – e.g. Scandinavia – where participation routes are more established and young people have more direct access to policy makers.

Interview with Saima Tarapdar, a young researcher, about her experiences of doing research

The following interview with Saima Tarapdar is an opportunity to hear from a young person about the experiences of being a young researcher and the potential for research by young people to influence policy. Saima has carried out several research projects. You can read her study about young carers '*I don't think people know enough about me and they don't care: Understanding and exploring the needs of young carers from their perspective*' on the Children's Research Centre website at http://childrens-research-centre.open.ac.uk [accessed 24/01/09].

Mary: What was it that interested you about becoming a young researcher?

Saima: I wanted to become a young researcher because I had many questions that needed answering and was critical of evidence around me. I started studying Sociology at GCSE, and it opened my eyes to the fact that some of my questions could be answered by doing research; from conducting an opinion poll in class about who my peers thought would win Pop Idol, to analysing the effect of classroom teaching aids on educational attainment. Most importantly, it also taught me that research uncovered more questions than answers and finding solutions to society's problems was far more complex than I had imagined.

One of the pivotal moments for me was completing the Young Researchers training programme with the Children's Research Centre (CRC) at the Open University. This gave me a new set of skills and I realised that I really could do some important research that might make a difference. I also realised that society was more ready to value what young people have to say. After doing the research training, the CRC supported me to do some research about the experiences of young carers. I am a young carer myself and found I was able to establish rapport easily with other young carers and ask questions on personal and sensitive topics about their roles and how they thought social policy could be changed to improve their life experiences. The tool of peer-to-peer interviews helped me gain access to rich qualitative data and showed me that as a young researcher I was able to uncover new information about the 'informal care' part of being a young carer.

Mary: What do you think society can learn from young people's research?

Saima: My experience has shown me that being a researcher is a role that can be conducted at any age. Young researchers are an untapped potential since they are not only capable of shedding light on topical issues relevant to and about young people but they also have valuable perspectives about issues not exclusive to youth. For example I did some research investigating issues of isolation and loneliness amongst elderly people in care homes and those in independent living accommodation. This information was then used to develop an elderly befriending scheme in my local area.

Mary: Just returning to children and young people for a moment, do you think young people's research can inform policy and practice about childhoods?

Saima: I definitely think it can! Young people want a platform to investigate issues that are of concern to them. They can produce high quality research and can make a valuable contribution to policy about children and young people's lives. One of the big issues in modern childhoods is having no space to do your own thing. All the spaces are controlled by adults. That's how so many young people just end up hanging around the streets and then we get more street crime. Earlier this year, I had the privilege of working with some young people who have special educational needs. We conducted a quantitative study asking young people (including young people with learning difficulties) and local residents how they could make their streets safer and how the police and local authorities could work with gangs to tackle street crime. We interviewed local gang members to understand what it was like to be part of a gang and how their experiences might lead us to a better understanding of the causes of street crime. Our peer-to-peer research was used to advantage to gain access to hard-to-reach young people and to interview shy young people. In doing this we were able to counter some of the negative media stereotypes about young people. I think the research we did made a difference in our local area and has made a contribution to the bigger policy debate about young people and street crime.

Pause for thought

In her interview, Saima touched on several themes that are central to this chapter and to the book more generally. She evidenced the advantage of her youth status in accessing peer–peer data impermeable to adults. She emphasized the valuable contributions that research by young people can make to policy such as the research she described about gangs and street crime. She showed how insights from research by young people can help change attitudes e.g. overturning the media stereotyping of young people. Young researchers like Saima can help take our thinking into new places and open up new possibilities.

Key points

- Research by children and young people can access peer-to-peer perspectives which offer important contributions to policy and practice.
- Much research carried out by children and young people is small scale and local. We need to do more to make these studies visible so that their findings can be applied to other settings and to larger policy arenas.

Summary

This chapter has:

- Examined the relationship between child research and politics and how this can temper the impact of research on policy and practice.
- Explored how research involving children can impact on policy and practice regarding childhoods and provided some examples.
- Considered how child research is impacting on childhood policies at a global level and reflected on the changes being brought about by the growth of cyberspace.
- Featured an interview with a young researcher.
- Discussed the extent to which research by children and young people can bring about change.

Final pause for thought: make it count!

During the lifetime of someone turning 21 this year, there will have been 98 separate Acts of Parliament passed across the UK that affect the services they use, 82 different strategies for various areas of children and youth services, 77 initiatives and over 50 new funding streams. That equals over 400 different major announcements – around 20 every year – with each new initiative lasting, on average, a little over two years. (Action for Children. 2008, p. 2)

With around 400 policy pronouncements typically affecting each generation of children, the potential for causing harm by getting it wrong certainly focuses the mind. Quality child research that informs our understanding of contemporary childhoods can help us get it right. We need to make it count! There could never be a more important – or more urgent – time for a rethinking of child research and how it can be used to optimize life chances for all our children, present and future.

Suggested further reading

Alexander, R. J. and Flutter, J. (2009) *Towards a New Primary Curriculum: [Interim] Report from the Cambridge Primary Review*, Cambridge: University of Cambridge Faculty of Education. Available at www.primaryreview.org.uk/downloads [accessed 27/03/09] or you can find it by keying 'Alexander report' into a search engine.

Rose, J. (2009) *The Independent Review of the Primary Curriculum*, www.numicon.com/Assets/Downloadablefile/IPRC_Report-15707.pdfRose report [accessed 27/03/09] or you can find it by keying 'Rose report' into a search engine.

Montgomery, H. and Kellett, M. (2009) (eds) *Children and Young People's Worlds: Frameworks for Developing Integrated Practice*, Bristol: Policy Press.

An edited volume containing chapters which discuss different issues affecting contemporary childhoods and childhood policies.

Thomas, N. (2002) *Children, Family and the State: Decision-making and Child Participation*, Bristol: The Policy Press.

A scholarly discussion exploring the connection between children, politics and policy making.

References

Action for Children (2008) *As Long as It Takes: A New Politics for Children*, London: Action for Children. www.actionforchildren.org [accessed 21/03/09].

Alanen, L. (1992) 'Modern childhood? Exploring the "child question" in sociology', *Publication Series A. Research Reports 50*, Jyvaskyla: University of Jyvaskyla, Institute for Educational Research.

Alderson, P. and Morrow, V. (2004) *Ethics, Social Research and Consulting with Children and Young People* (2nd edn), Ilford: Barnado's.

Alexander, R. J. and Flutter, J. (2009) *Towards a New Primary Curriculum: [Interim] Report from the Cambridge Primary Review*, Cambridge: University of Cambridge Faculty of Education. Available at www.primaryreview.org.uk/downloads [accessed 27/03/09].

Anning, A., Cottrell, D., Frost, N., Green, J. and Robinson, M. (2006) *Developing Multiprofessional Teamwork for Integrated Children's Services*, Maidenhead: Open University Press.

Ataov, A. and Haider, J. (2006) 'From participation to empowerment: critical reflections on a participatory action research project with street children in Turkey', *Children Youth and Environments*, 16, 2, 127–152.

Bandura, A., Ross, D. and Ross S. (1961) 'Transmission of aggression through imitation of aggressive models', *Journal of Abnormal and Social Psychology*, 63, 575–582.

Barker, R. (2008) *Making Sense of Every Child Matters: Multi-professional Practice Guidance*, Bristol: Policy Press.

Breggin, P. (1998) *Talking Back to Ritalin: What Doctors Aren't Telling You about Stimulants for Children*, Monroe: Common Courage Press.

Buckingham, D. and Bragg, S. (2009) 'Children and consumer culture'. In Montgomery, H. and Kellett, M. (eds) *Children and Young People's Worlds: Developing Frameworks for Integrated Practice*, Bristol: Policy Press, pp. 181–198.

Bucknall, S. (2008) 'Students as researchers: exploring distributed leadership in a school context', London: ESRC National Centre for Research Methods Seminar.

Burman, E. (1994) *Deconstructing Developmental Psychology*, London: Routledge.

Chawla, L. (ed.) (2002) *Growing up in an Urbanising World*, Paris and London: UNESCO Publishing/ Earthscan Publications.

Christensen, P. and Prout, A. (2002) 'Working with ethical symmetry in social research with children', *Childhood*, 9, 4, 477–497.

—(2005) 'Anthropological and sociological perspectives on the study of children'. In Greene, S. and Hogan, D. (eds) *Researching Children's Experiences: Approaches and Methods*, London: Sage, pp. 42–60.

Clark, A. and Moss, P. (2001) *Listening to Young Children: The Mosaic Approach*, London: National Children's Bureau.

—(2005) *Spaces to Play: More Listening to Young Children Using the Mosaic Approach*, London: National Children's Bureau.

Clark, C., Ghosh, A., Green, E. and Shariff, N. (2009) *Media Portrayal of Young People – Impact and Influences*, www.nya.org/yrn [accessed 23/03/09].

Coppock, V. (2002) 'Medicalising children's behaviour'. In Franklin, B. (ed.) *The New Handbook of Children's Rights: Comparative Policy and Practice*, New York: Routledge, pp. 139–154.

Cross, B. (2002) 'Children's stories negotiated identities; Bakhtim and complexity in upper primary classrooms in Jamaica and Scotland', PhD Thesis: Edinburgh University.

Cunningham, H. (2006) *The Invention of Childhood*, London: BBC Books.

Davey, C. (2009) *What Do They Know?*, www.crae.org.uk [accessed 11/02/09].

Davis, J. M. (2009) *Life of a Disabled Child*, www.leeds.ac.uk/disability-studies/projects/children.htm [accessed 06/02/09].

Devine, D. (2002) 'Children's citizenship and the structuring of adult–child relations in the primary school', *Childhood*, 9, 3, 303–320.

Department for Children, Schools and Families (2007) *Consolidated Third and Fourth Report to the UN Committee on the Rights of the Child*, London: HMSO.

—(2008) *Children's Plan*, London: HMSO.

Department for Education and Skills (2003) *Every Child Matters*, Green Paper, London: HMSO.

—(2005) *Youth Matters*, London: HMSO.

—(2006) *Youth Matters: Next Steps*, London: HMSO.

Farrell, A. (2005) (ed.) *Ethical Research with Children*, Maidenhead: Open University Press.

Franklin, B. (2002) *The New Handbook of Children's Rights: Comparative policy and practice*, London: Routledge.

Gallagher, M. (2009) 'Researching the geography of power in a primary school'. In Tisdall, K., Davis, J. and Gallagher, M. (eds) *Researching with Children and Young People: Research Design, Methods and Analysis*, London: Sage, pp. 57–64.

Gillick v West Norfolk and Wisbech Area Health Authority (1985) 3 All ER 402 HL, http://www.law-campus.butterworths.com/student/Lev3/weblinked_books/fortin/dataitem.asp?ID=12595&tid=7 [accessed 23/03/07].

Gramsci, A. (1971) *Selections from the Prison Notebooks*, New York: International Publishers.

Gray, D. E. and Denicolo, P. (1998) 'Research in special needs education: objectivity or ideology?', *British Journal of Special Education*, 25, 3, 140–145.

Greene, S. and Hill, M. (2005) 'Researching children's experience: methods and methodological issues'. In Greene, S. and Hogan, D. (eds) *Researching Children's Experience: Approaches and Methods*, London: Sage, pp. 1–22.

Griesel, D., Swart-Kruger, J. and Chawla, L. (2004) 'Children in South Africa can make a difference: an assessment of "Growing Up in Cities" in Johannesburg'. In Fraser, S. et al. (eds) *The Reality of*

Research with Children and Young People, London: Sage in association with Open University Press, pp. 277–295.

Hallett, C. and Prout, A. (2003) (eds) *Hearing the Voices of Children: Social Policy for a New Century*, London and New York: Routledge Falmer.

Hamill, P. and Boyd, B. (2002) 'Equality, fairness and rights – the young person's voice', *British Journal of Special Education*, 29, 3, 111–117.

Hartas, D. (2008) *The Right to Childhoods*, London: Continuum.

Hendrick, H. (1997) 'Constructions and reconstructions of British childhood: an interpretive survey, 1800 to present'. In James, A. and Prout, A. (1997) (eds) *Constructing and Reconstructing Childhood* (2nd edn), Basingstoke: Falmer Press, pp. 34–62.

—(2000) 'The child as social actor in historical sources: problems of identification and interpretation'. In Christensen, P. and James, A. (eds) *Research with Children and Young People: Perspectives and Practices*, London: RoutledgeFalmer, pp. 36–61.

Hill, M. (2005) 'Ethical considerations in researching children's experiences'. In Greene, S. and Hogan, D. (eds) *Researching Children's Experience*, London: Sage, pp. 61–86.

Information Centre for Research in Health and Social Care (2007) *Report on Young People's Mental Health*, Information Centre for Research in Health and Social Care University of Bristol.

James, A. (1999) 'Researching children's social competence: methods and models'. In Woodhead, M., Faulkner, D. and Littleton. K. (eds) *Making Sense of Social Development*, London: Routledge in association with The Open University, pp. 231–249.

James, A., Jenks, C. and Prout, A. (1998) *Theorizing Childhood*, Cambridge: Polity Press.

Jans, M. (2004) 'Children as citizens: towards a contemporary notion of child participation', *Childhood*, 11, 1, 27–44.

Jones, A. (2004) 'Involving children and young people as researchers'. In Fraser, S., Lewis, V., Ding, S., Kellett, M. and Robinson, C. (eds) *Doing Research with Children and young People*, London: Sage in association with Open University Press, pp. 113–130.

Jones, A., Jeyashingham, D. and Rajasooriya, S. (2002) *Invisible Families: The Strengths and Needs of Black Families in Which Young People Have Caring Responsibilities*, Bristol: Policy Press.

Kellett, M. (2001) 'Jacob's journey: developing sociability and communication in a young boy with severe and complex learning difficulties using the Intensive Interaction teaching approach', *Journal of Research in Special Educational Needs*, 3, 1, 18–34.

—(2005) *How to Develop Children as Researchers: A Step by Step Guide to Teaching Research Process*, London: Paul Chapman.

—(2005a) 'Children as active researchers: a new research paradigm for the 21st century?' Published online by ESRC National Centre for Research Methods, NCRM/003 www.ncrm.ac.uk/publications [accessed 17/01/09].

Layard, R. and Dunn, J. (2009) *A Good Childhood*, London: Penguin.

Lazos, H. D. (2002) *Playing in Time: Ancient Greek and Byzantine Games*, Athens: Aiolos Publishing.

Lenzer, G. (2002) 'Children's studies and the human rights of children: toward a unified approach'. In Alaimo, K. and Klug, B. (eds) *Children as Equals – Exploring the Rights of the Child*, Lanham, MD: University Press of America, pp. 207–225.

Lloyd-Smith, M. and Tarr, J. (2000) 'Researching children's perspectives: a sociological dimension'. In Lewis, A. and Lindsay, G. (eds) *Researching Children's Perspectives*, Buckingham: Open University Press, pp. 59–70.

Lundy, L. (2007) '"Voice" is not enough: conceptualising Article 12 of the United Nations Convention on the Rights of the Child', *British Educational Research Journal*, 33, 6, 927–942.

Mason, J. and Tipper, B. (2008) 'Being related: how children define and create kinship', *Childhood*, 15, 4, 441–460.

Mayall, B. (2000) 'Conversations with children: working with generational issues'. In Christensen, P. and James, A. (eds) *Research with Children: Perspectives and Practices*, London: Routledge Falmer, pp. 120–135.

McDonald, K. (2007) 'The importance of identity in policy: the case for and of children'. Paper presented at the Suicide Prevention Resource Centre workshop, Australia: University of South Wales.

Mead, M. (1928) *Coming of Age in Samoa: A Psychological Study of Primitive Youth for Western Civilisation*, New York: Dell.

—(1930) *Growing up in New Guinea*, New York: Morrow Quill Paperbacks.

Meadows, S., Herrick, D. and Witt, M. (2008) 'Improvement in national test arithmetic scores at Key Stage 1: grade inflation or better achievements?', *Educational Research*, 34, 4, 491–503.

Mental Health Foundation (1998) *The Big Picture: Promoting Children and Young People's Health*, London: Mental Health Foundation.

Montgomery, H. (2009) *An Introduction to Childhood: Anthropological Perspectives on Children's Lives*, Oxford: Blackwell.

Montgomery, H. and Kellett, M. (2009) (eds) *Children and Young People's Worlds: Frameworks for Developing Integrated Practice*, Bristol: Policy Press.

Morrow, V. and Richards M. (1996) 'The ethics of social research with children: an overview', *Children & Society*, 10, 2, 90–105.

Mullis, I. V. S., Martin, M. O., Kennedy, A. M. and Foy, P. (2007) *Progress in International Reading Literacy Study (PIRLS) in Primary School in 40 Countries*, Chestnut Hill, MA: TIMSS & PIRLS International Study Center, Boston College.

Nieuwenhuys, O. (2001) 'By the sweat of their brow? Street children, NGOs and children's rights in Addis Ababa', *Africa*, 71, 4, 539–557.

O'Byrne, D. J. (2003) *Human Rights: An Introduction*. London: Pearson Education

Ong, A. (2006) 'Mutations in citizenship', *Theory, Culture and Society*, 23, (2–3), 499–505.

Orme, C. (2008) *What People in My School and Community Think about the Police*, http://childrens-research-centre.open.ac.uk [accessed 10/11/09].

Pandya, R. (2007) 'Working with young refugees and asylum seekers through participatory action research in health promotion'. In Sallah, M. and Howson, C. (eds) *Working with Black Young People*, Lyme Regis: Russell House Publishing, pp. 123–134.

Parker, S. (1997) *Reflective Teaching in the Postmodern World*, Buckingham: Open University Press.

Pollard, A. and Triggs, P. (2000) *What Pupils Say: Policy and Practice in Primary Education*, London: Continuum.

Punch, K. F. (2005) *Introduction to Social Research Methods: Quantitative and Qualitative Approaches* (2nd edn), London: Sage.

Punch, S. (2004) 'Negotiating autonomy: children's use of time and space in rural Bolivia'. In Lewis, V., Kellett, M., Robinson, C., Fraser, S. and Ding, S. (eds) *The Reality of Research with Children and Young People*, London: Sage in association with Open University Press, pp. 94–115.

Rose, J. (2009) *The Independent Review of the Primary Curriculum* www.numicon.com/Assets/ Downloadablefile/IPRC_Report-15707.pdfRose report [accessed 27/03/09].

Rhodes, H., Mark, L. and Perry, T. (2007) *Children's Attitudes to Literacy Homework*, http://childrens-research-centre.open.ac.uk [accessed 10/11/09].

Sainsbury, M. and Schagen, I. (2004) *Attitudes towards Reading at Ages Nine to Eleven, Journal of Research in Reading*, 27, 4, 373–386.

Sandaek, M. and Einarsson, J. H. (2008) *Children and Young People's Report to the UN on Their Rights: Annex to Norway's Fourth Report on the Convention on the Rights of the Child*, www.childwatch.uio. no/publications [accessed 04/04/09].

Schein, E. and Bernstein, P. (2007) *Identical Strangers*, New York: Random House.

Shakespeare, T. (1996) 'Rules of engagement: doing disability research', *Disability*, 11, 1, 115–119.

Sturman, L. (2003) 'Teaching to the tests: science or intuition?', *Educational Research*, 45, 3, 261–273.

Taylor, S. A. (2000) 'The UN Convention on the Rights of the Child'. In Lewis, A. and Lindsay, G. (eds) *Researching Children's Perspectives*, Buckingham: Open University Press, pp. 21–33.

Taylor, N. J., Smith, A. B. and Gollop, M. (2008) 'New Zealand children and young people's perspectives on citizenship', *The International Journal of Children's Rights*, 16, 2, 195–210.

Thomas, N. (2002) *Children, Family and the State: Decision-making and Child Participation*, Bristol: The Policy Press.

Thorne, B. (2002) 'From silence into voice: bringing children more fully into knowledge', *Childhood*, 9, 3, 251–254.

Tudge, J. R. H., and Hogan, D. (2005) 'An ecological approach to observations of children's everyday lives'. In Greene. S. and Hogan, D. (eds) *Researching Children's Experience: Approaches and Methods*, London: Sage, pp. 102–121.

Tudge, J. R. H., Hogan, D. and Etz, K. (1999) 'Using naturalistic observations as a window into children's everyday lives: an ecological approach'. In Berardo, F. M. (series ed.) and Shehan, C. (vol. ed.) *Contemporary Perspectives on Family Research, Vol 1. Through the Eyes of the Child: Re-visioning Children as Active Agents of Family Life*, Stamford, CT: JAI Press, pp. 109–132.

UNICEF United Nations Children's Fund (2007) *Child Poverty in Perspective: An Overview of Child Well-being in Rich Countries*, Florence: UNICEF Innocenti Research Centre.

—(2008) *Knowing Children*, Bangkok: UNICEF Thailand.

United Nations Convention on the Rights of the Child (1989) Geneva: United Nations.

United Nations High Commission for Refugees (2007) *Protecting Refugees*, Geneva: UNHCR publication.

Van Krieken, R. (1992) *Children and the State: Social Control and the Formation of Australian Child Welfare*, Sydney: Allen & Unwin.

—(1999) 'The "stolen generations" and cultural genocide: the forced removal of Australian Indigenous children from their families and its implications for the sociology of childhood', *Childhood*, 6, 3, 297–311.

Veale, A. (2005) 'Creative methodologies in research with children and young people'. In Greene S. and Hogan D. (eds) *Researching Children's Experience: Approaches and Methods*, London: Sage, pp. 253–272.

Waller, T. (2006) '"Don't come too close to my octopus tree": recording and evaluating young children's perspectives on outdoor learning', *Children, Youth and Environments*, 16, 2, 75–104.

Warming, H. (2006) '"How can you know? You're not a foster child": dilemmas and possibilities of giving voice to children in foster care', *Children, Youth and Environments*, 16, 2, 28–50.

Wenger, E. (1998) *Communities of Practice*, Cambridge: Cambridge University Press.

Westcott, H. and Littleton, K. (2000) 'Exploring meaning in interviews with children'. In Greene, S. and Hogan, D. (eds) *Researching Children's Experience: Approaches and Methods*, London: Sage, pp. 141–158.

Woodhead, M. and Faulkner, D. (2008) 'Subjects, objects or participants? Dilemmas of psychological research with children'. In Christensen, P. and James, A. (eds) *Research with Children: Perspectives and Practice* (2nd edn), Abingdon: Routledge, pp. 10–39.

World Health Organisation (2001) *World Health Report*, Geneva: World Health Organisation.

Index